Praise for *Grimoire of the Thorn*

"When we open ourselves to the presence of Holy Nature, a different kind of magic happens. Raven Grimassi shows us a gateway, a path, and a way of integration with the realms of enchantment that are right in front of us, if we but know where to look and have the patience to watch, listen, and learn."

—T. THORN COYLE, author of *Make Magic of Your Life* and *Kissing the Limitless*

"It has often been said that a good witch uses what works. Moreover, many in the broader magickal community extol the value of being in living religions that continue to evolve and change with the times. What Raven Grimassi has created in this book is a system of Witchcraft as fresh as your next breath and as old as the dreams of your ancestors that slumber in your blood. The Rose and Thorn Path is truly inspired and is a vision that has been refined by the decades of Raven Grimassi's work into a Path that many will find as authentic and genuine. Virtually everything that we have today started in the inner realms of bards, prophets, and seers long before they were recorded and became official lore and writ."

—Ivo DOMINGUEZ, author of *Casting Sacred Space*

"Raven Grimassi has brought us the ultimate treasure—that thing for which we've searched so long but failed to unearth: the missing link that connects all magical systems and makes each one viable. Undoubtedly, it's the most exciting and important book of the decade!"

—DOROTHY MORRISON, author of *Utterly Wicked* and *The Craft*

"Behold a spirited piece of work exploring the underlying mystical currents of Witchcraft. As Mr. Grimassi encourages a tossing-out of titles and pretenses, he dually encourages readers to embrace their abilities as Natural Witches—nature mystics who understand the parallels of human consciousness and the earth's regenerative flora. While the mythos, names, and rituals of the Rose and Thorn Path may be inspired by modern vision, its essence is as old as the turning tides around us."

—RAVEN DIGITALIS, author of *Shadow Magick Compendium*
and *Empathy*

"I have always loved Raven Grimassi's writings. It is a pleasure when I see him at festivals and hear that a new book is out. *The Grimoire of the Thorn-Blooded Witch* is no exception. From a spiritual point of view this book gives the reader a new thought pattern to follow in the journey from birth to death. As a wood worker and wielder of spiritual energies through vascular plants I found his detailed work on Plant Spirits to be most enlightening. Further I was impressed by his work with two tools often ignored in many magical tomes: the Mortar and Pestle. It is evident through this section that Raven has an intimate knowledge of the workings of magical plants and how to combine and/or separate those energies where needed. This is essential in all crafts and is too many times given passing comments instead of in-depth review. The final sections are of the Old Ones and their Rites. These sections were well thought out, well presented, and the reader could see where the author was coming from and going to; something that is often missed in many books on our subjects. There is reverence in Raven's writings and of all places it shows deepest in these last few chapters."

—GYPSEY ELAINE TEAGUE, author of *Steampunk Magick*

"Deeply moving and traditional with historic integrity, Grimassi's book introducing the reader to the Path of the Rose and Thorn is also deeply personal to the author. Abundant with references to historians, energized with numerous deities, the books is a garden unto itself. Grimassi presents the text in a thoughtful manner, guiding the reader through the spiritual construct and cosmology of the tradition to the acquisition of the appropriate ritual tools with beautiful rituals for their consecration. Grimassi further guides you into the deeper Mysteries of the Green World, introducing you to those species most important to this Path, and then through the ritual calendar. This is one of those books which is likely to change your life (for the better)."

—REV. PAUL BEYERL at The Hermit's Grove, author of *The Master Book of Herbalism*

"With this enigmatic entry into the occult lore, Raven Grimassi reminds us that true Witchcraft resonates within the hidden tides of the natural world, where those energies connect to the very essence of the human soul. Many books talk about the relationship of Witches to natural magic. This book takes you into the very heart of it through myth, rituals and communion with the gods of old, those ancient spirits discovered within the deepest wood and enchanted garden."

—CHRISTIAN DAY, author of *The Witches' Book of the Dead*

"It is rare to find a witch who has the courage and prescience to journey the winding path and return with an understanding that is beyond their own ego. Raven Grimassi proves to be that rare witch. In *Grimoire of the Thorn-Blooded Witch*, Raven takes us on a journey climbing down the ladder into the depths of the soul of nature and back up into the stars themselves. He has given us a grimoire which speaks to mysteries that are deeply old with an understanding that is richly new. He clearly reveals philosophy, but does not stop there, instead bringing us into practical application as well. Truly a work of genius, *Grimoire of the Thorn-Blooded Witch* promises to become a classic read."

—ANDREW THEITIC, executive editor of *The Witches' Almanac*

"*Grimoire of the Thorn-Blooded Witch* is a landmark book of witch-ery! Grimassi has invited us into a world where the lines between human and other, seen and unseen, deep and height, shadow and light meet revealing the potent and primal currents of witchery. As a Traditional Witch, Southern Conjure-Man and Faery Seer, I *know* the power and wisdom that comes when a human partners with the spirit of 'other' and thus, reveals the ancient wisdom that flows from the living memory of our planet, the soul of the earth. That power and wisdom is accessible through the treasures in this book. Bring the mysteries of your red blood to the mysteries of the green blood, and awaken the Thorn-Blooded Witch within you. The underworld powers of magical alchemy await within these pages!"

—Orion Foxwood, author of *The Candle and the Crossroads*

"In your hands is Raven Grimassi's most personal and powerful work to date. In it he shares profound Craft teachings that will transform your relationship with magick, and your work as a Witch. I wish I'd had access to this treasure earlier on my path."

—Christopher Penczak, co-Founder of the Temple of Witch-craft and author of the *Plant Spirit Familiar*

Grimoire

OF THE

THORN-BLOODED WITCH

Grimoire

OF THE

THORN-BLOODED WITCH

MASTERING THE FIVE ARTS OF OLD WORLD WITCHERY

RAVEN GRIMASSI

WEISERBOOKS

San Francisco, CA / Newburyport, MA

First published in 2014 by Weiser Books
Red Wheel/Weiser, LLC
With offices at:
665 Third Street, Suite 400
San Francisco, CA 94107
www.redwheelweiser.com

ISBN: 978-1-57863-550-4

Library of Congress Cataloging-in-Publication Data available upon request.

Interior illustrations by Jane Starr Weils
Cover design by Jim Warner
Cover image: Surreal portrait of woman by Giuseppe Arcimboldo, oil on wood, circa 1591, 1527–1593, Private Collection, © Fine Art Images / SuperStock
Interior by Maureen Forys, Happenstance Type-O-Rama
Typeset in Historical Fell, IM Fell Great Primer Pro, and Goudy Text MT

Printed in the United States of America.
EBM
10 9 8 7 6 5 4

To the Rose that unfurled in the center of
my world, who inspires me and sustains my
will to reach the unreachable star.

CONTENTS

PREFACE

Many years have passed since I first began to write about my experience of Witchcraft and to teach what I understood about it. Naturally, all of this has grown and evolved over time. Although I've been taught by other Witches along the way, I eventually formed relationships with the spirits of moon and night, and these had a profound influence on me. Others before me certainly had the same experience and understanding of such a connection. I believe that this is how our ancestors came to obtain knowledge of mystical and hidden things. It's not an invention by an individual; it's a revealing to one from something outside. It comes through an alignment that establishes communication with beings dwelling in nonmaterial reality.

I first came into contact with the Rose and Thorn Path of Witchery through conversations with Old World Witches whom I met by way of the opportunities that being an author can provide. This made it possible for me to meet key people in occult circles. Additionally, I came into contact with various individuals who wrote me letters that were inspired by my books and articles. I hasten to add that none of these passed the system on to me but were instead instrumental to me in finding the enchanted garden of the Rose and Thorn.

Over the years, I was guided to meet other practitioners of related paths through my network of authors, festival coordinators, and event planners. From them, I learned a variety of concepts and techniques that eventually led me to this particular expression of the Greenwood Realm, that is to say, the Ways of the Rose and Thorn. It was there in the center of the enchanted garden that I met the deepest core of teachers; they are the spirits of plants and the spirits of places. It was here in direct contact with the deep places within the Greenwood that very profound things were revealed to me.

When I first encountered the Path of the Rose and Thorn, I arrived with four decades of experience in various forms of Witchcraft and Wicca. I see now that this was a necessary foundation for me in order to be receptive to an expanded vision and a needed change. This change came about by releasing my adherence to any specific cultural form of Witchcraft. When I left behind my finite connections, I became open to the formless ways that preceded them. I fell back into the brewing cauldron from which all things emerge. When I surfaced, my self-identity as a Witch of any specific cultural expression of Witchcraft had dissolved away. I felt closer to the larger concept of Witch than to being *a* Witch singled out by cultural imprint. This release from a lifelong identity was one of powerful transformation and liberation.

I don't regard my detachment from a cultural definition of my Witchcraft as an abandoning of my previous Path. Instead, I regard the Rose and Thorn Path as a means of expanding upon its enchanted world–view. The Old Path of Witchery is about rootedness, and beneath the surface, it runs a network of currents that feed traditions. These traditions rise from it and recede back into it over time. Nothing is ever forgotten at the rooted level even though the exterior forms may die away over time.

The Ancestral Spirit speaks to us from the blood flowing through our veins, for it contains the memory of our lineage. There are other voices willing to inform us, and they whisper in the quiet times when we are receptive. We are connected to them when our spirits embrace the same things. A kindred connection forms when we emanate with the love of the plant realm, when we sense the moon's light as sacred, and when we understand Nature as self-aware. These are the stepping stones that lead from the Witches' garden to the threshold of the Otherworld.

What I offer you in this book isn't about faith or belief; it's about experiences. Through those experiences, I have come to know and to realize. This is very different from dealing with faith or holding to beliefs. To this I add my long-acquired understanding of Witchcraft, one that was not easily formed or attained. It came at great cost to me, and I've endured much in my personal and professional life to hold true to the Ways.

My past experiences have proven to me that there are people who don't want you to know that they do not know. So they hide it through distraction in the form of criticizing other individuals. There are people who hold ill will toward others who have done the work and achieved the things that they have not, dreamers who never put forth the effort required to attain them in their own lives. My book is not for them. It's for you who realize that the thorns are worth the attainment of the rose.

The pages that lie ahead in this book are filled with the meadows of old lore. With each one, you walk the rustic paths leading into the deep wooded places. If you are open to it, moonlight will reflect from the written word. There's enchantment to be found. Awaiting you are the old spirits who can part the thickets, reveal the thresholds to what lies beyond, and dance with you all through the moonlit night in a realm few mortals know.

INTRODUCTION

There are timeless things that refuse to remain silent and unknown. They speak through human vessels, even those that are flawed. An ancient spirit presses on, perseveres, and is carried upon the current that flows through time. It will not be denied; it will not be muted. In this book, you will find persistent themes that feel right to the inner spirit. They are markers leading back in time as they trace ancient memories.

I remember reading somewhere that author J. R. R. Tolkien, of *The Lord of the Rings* fame, reportedly commented that he wasn't writing fiction; he was writing forgotten history. I'm not suggesting that what he wrote has any historical merit, but I want to point out how powerful mythical history is despite its lack of a foundation in what we call reality. Beliefs in ancient forgotten worlds, mystical beings, and fabled creatures of all kinds existed long before anyone wrote anything of a historical nature.

The things of prehistory, and of nonhistorical value, persist in the beloved tales that inspire and entertain us. They have as much impact on us today as anything historical, and perhaps even more so. It seems they convey something that our spirits understand and hold to be true in a way that our intellect can't surrender to completely. As the saying goes, just because something is only in your mind doesn't mean it isn't real.

Unlike many of my previous books, in this one, I don't argue for anything historical nor do I present an alternative history. This is a book about practices, techniques, and ways related to the practice of Witchcraft as a means of working with the Greenwood Realm. Its purpose is to turn our understanding of Witchcraft back to something more primal in nature than the modern forms we read about in popular books today. I place importance on the roots of Witchcraft instead of on the new flowers growing on the old tree, so to speak.

The magical system presented in this book is ever ancient and ever new. Although I've known it in various forms and at various levels, until just a few years ago, it's never been one cohesive system (at least not as presented in the following pages). That being said, we must not lose sight of the fact that basic elements of this magical system have existed since ancient times. This is only important in the sense of roots. It's the roots that provide nourishment.

It was in the year 2006 that I fully embraced the roots of the Rose and Thorn Path. This required trusting in a magical process, one that proved entirely worthy of that trust. It began with the rose, or more specifically with an entity connected to it. This entity is called She of the Thorn-Blooded Rose. It's a very old idea that spirits inhabit plants, trees, and other things within Nature. Therefore, it was nothing alien to my practice of Witchcraft for me to make contact with the spirits linked to the rose. I had communicated with plant spirits long before this opportunity but never to the depth that proved to be the case with She of the Thorn-Blooded Rose.

Her title is connected to the theme of the covenant of the blood, which is based upon the exchange of a few drops of human blood and plant blood. Blood is the essence of the life force, and the intimacy of its sharing is a very powerful bonding. To that end, I obtained some liquid chlorophyll, which is the green blood of plants. Interestingly, a year or two prior to this work, drinking chlorophyll was prescribed to me by a natural healer as a remedy for some very odd symptoms that were plaguing my health at the time.

Part of my initial work with the Rose and Thorn Path was to acquire a rose bush. It was to be used as the sacred connection to She of the Thorn-Blooded Rose, and eventually to all the spirits of the plants used in Witchcraft. More importantly, it became the root system through which the organic memory of the earth could be tapped directly. This is the idea that all living things of the past released their essence into the soil through decomposition. Their memories are held within the crystalline composition of the minerals in the soil. In the Rose and Thorn Path, minerals are called the bones of the earth. In this light, we can tap into the bone memory of the earth.

I planted the rose bush in my yard and dedicated it to She of the Thorn-Blooded Rose. I then performed the simple rite of offering three drops of blood mixed with water. The offering was slowly and reverently poured upon the crown of the bush, which is at the base of the plant. I then poured out a small portion of the green blood, spent a few moments connecting with the idea of this as the entity's blood, and then drank it.

Across from my home, at the time, there stood a strip of woods surrounding a ravine. The locals call such a place the Dingle. It was always pleasant to watch the wildlife come and go through this area. Within a few days of the rose bush ritual, a pattern and a practice developed for me. I found that sitting on my porch in the early morning became a time of transmission, and the period of dusk was a time of interpretation and integration. Just like plant life, I was beginning to respond to sunlight and its diminishment in ways that I had not previously done.

As the sun awakened the Greenwood, something was openly and purposefully communicating with me. Part of my previous training was in maintaining a mental balance in my work with mystical realities so as to not allow either the worldly or the mystical to override one another. Therefore, I was able to discern that this wasn't fantasy or wishful thinking.

In the beginning, most of what was communicated wasn't all that new or alien. Through that inner voice that we all hear, I listened to the teachings about the sentient nature of the woods. This began to expand upon the concept of the Forest having a mind, and that the leaves of the trees were, in effect, cells in that brain. From there it turned to a communication that the leaves are separate beings, and for lack of a better term, I came to call them the leaf people. My intellect looked at this as a metaphor, but my spirit felt a truth that took a while to settle in. It came in the Fall season as the leaves began to drop. The leaf people were abandoning their bodies and retreating into the tree branches. They would be reborn in the buds of the Spring season. It was nonsense that made complete sense.

I began to keep a notebook with me when I sat on the porch and watched the Dingle. It quickly began to be filled with teachings and the transmission of symbols. Odd drawings were guided onto the pages, along with words that didn't belong to any language of which I had any knowledge. They came at first without context or relevance. The Otherworldliness of it all was inescapable. As a well-experienced practitioner of Witchcraft, I knew enough to be an observer of the process and a gatherer of elements. Discernment would come later as the pieces began to reveal a portrait.

Over a period of two months, I found that faces were forming in the bark of the trunks of the trees. Visitors noticed them too, without any prompting or beforehand conversation. Some of the faces were friendly, almost comical, while others were not. The Dingle seemed to be releasing energy all around the foliage in the formation of blurry vaporous bands that outlined the plants and trees. Communication quickened.

With the writing of this book, I've now been working in this Path for six years. Many of the terms, phrases, and titles used in this book came from those sessions on the porch. There was, however, another form of communication that arose. It's called the passing on of Shadow, which most frequently happens in the dream state. In this realm of consciousness, there is no objection to things like being able to breathe underwater, fly through the sky, or have something you're holding turn into something else. It's the perfect setting for spirits to communicate in person, because in the Dream World, it's easily accepted that they can. In the waking state, they find humans quite difficult to talk with and far too resistant.

When you're successfully working with the plant spirits in this book, you will have visits and teaching sessions in the dream state, at least initially. This can and should shift to the waking state as well, although you'll likely find that experience less profound. In the meantime, keep a notebook at your bedside, and upon awakening write down your recollections and your thoughts at the time. Don't think about them—quickly record them. You'll eventually compose a dream-begotten grimoire of Greenwood magic.

Dreams are portals to the mystical realms of the soul; through them, we enter a realm without finite restrictions. The same is true of myths as they reveal to our spirits the truths that physical reality denies us. This is why the epic tales of the hero endure the Ages, for they allow us to recognize ourselves in a separate reality. In this, we believe that we could do what the hero did if our lives had turned out differently, if we weren't burdened with the things that limit us.

Two chapters in this book are devoted to mythical characters and themes within the Rose and Thorn Path. However, the beings that appear in the stories are also part of the *immortal race* that is embraced in our Path. In this regard, they're not fictional; it's the stories about them that are mythical. These tales are meant to preserve inner teachings that are woven into the myths and to connect occult themes together that are important within the teachings of the Rose and Thorn Path.

In these chapters, you'll be introduced to a host of plant spirits that are connected primarily to the traditional plants of Witchcraft. You'll also encounter the deities of the Path and discover that titles instead of names are used for them. One reason for this is that to place a name on a deity ties it to cultural setting. Doing so causes the deity to be seen through the limits of a specific cultural understanding and depiction. This finite reduction of the divine can be problematic. For example, there's a major difference between the title Goddess of the Moon and the name Selene, Goddess of the Moon. The former is expansive and all-inclusive; the latter is culturally defined and thereby excludes other cultural forms.

As you read through the chapters of this book, you'll encounter several key mystical elements. One that stands out is the idea of the Hallow. In occultism, reality is divided into material and nonmaterial dimensions. The idea of the Hallow is that a buffer exists between the dimensions. This zone is neither of the two in nature. It's a third reality and is in keeping with the occult importance of the number three and the presentation of triformis as one entity with three aspects.

Beyond the concepts in this book, what I want to share are the doorways they open. In working with other people of this Path, I have found it very confirming to observe their experiences. What we've connected with isn't fanciful. It's also not in keeping with things that are trendy, nor is it an elaboration or reworking of modern Wicca and Witchcraft. However, what it does share in common with them is inescapable because despite being modern practices, they do contain ancient elements or pieces as well. That being said, you will find one chapter on modern rites in the Rose and Thorn Path, which contains a Wheel of the Year–style collection of rites.

It's arguable that the model of a Wheel of the Year is a Wiccan concept. I don't personally regard it as a Wiccan copyright, and I note that many modern Pagans who don't call themselves Wiccans celebrate these seasonal rites. Whatever it is, whatever its origins may be, the Wheel of the Year is now an integral part of modern practice. Therefore, it seems important to include the associated rites of the seasons in this book for those wanting that connection to the larger Craft and Pagan communities.

For those readers solely interested in rites not attached to the Wheel of the Year or Wiccan themes in general, I have provided chapter 8, "The Old Rites." These will introduce you to ways of personal empowerment and will offer alignments to beings such as the Washer in the Night and the Three Daughters of Night. Also included is a rite known as Bearing the Witches' Trident. I believe these will prove not only to be refreshing; they will also help you claim your rightful power as a Witch.

Before closing this introduction to the book, I would be remiss not to include some words on the rose. It's a very important concept in the Path and has many facets that reflect its beauty and value within the system. The rose is a symbol of the inner mysteries of Witchcraft. A red rose symbolizes the mysteries as they reside in Nature, within the living things. The white rose symbolizes the Otherworld and the mysteries hidden in secret places. When a single rose appears with white petals in the center of red petals, this represents the mysteries joined together within one reality. Thorns appearing with the rose represent challenges and the dedication required to fully grasp the enlightenment of the rose.

One of the symbolisms associated with the rose reveals the covenant between the Witch and the Faery. In this, we find that both are stewards of the portal that opens to the inner mysteries. The Faery holds the celestial key, and the Witch bears the terrestrial key. When the two are joined together, they form an *X*—the sign of the crossroads. In this formation, where the keys cross we find a third point, the in-between place at the center. This is where the portal exists, and this is where it opens between the worlds.

Look at the shape of the *X* and you can see four pointed tip markers (the *V* shapes). The upper half of the *X* points down, and the lower half points up. On the sides of the *X*, you can see that the left and right halves point to the center. This shows us that when the celestial and terrestrial realms join, they pull together the left ways and the right ways. These are occult terms for esoteric and exoteric modes of consciousness. In the fusion, everything briefly loses its distinction, its ability to mask the opposite reality, and in doing so, the secret third reality emerges in the center of it all. If this sounds confusing or nonsensical, then the guardian of that portal is doing its job well.

The material in this book will connect you with an entity connected to the rose and its mystery. This is the previously mentioned She of the Thorn-Blooded Rose. With her guidance, you can be directed to the portal, and through it you can meet a variety of beings and entities. However, her primary task is to connect you with the Greenwood Realm and the plant spirits within it.

In your journey to encounter these spirits, you will pass through the organic memory of the earth. You'll walk upon roads of mystical concepts and be accompanied by the Old Ones of myth and legend. The moon and stars will bear witness. You need only embrace the best-known secret of all: no mystery is closed to an open mind.

What came of that mystical wedding, of the world
we know and the world we do not know, by that
rose of the spirit, committed thus in so great a
hope, so great a faith? The Druid is not here to
tell. Faith after Faith has withered like a leaf. But
still we stand by ancestral altars, still offer the
Rose of Desire to the veiled Mystery, still commit
this our symbol to the fathomless, the everlasting,
the unanswered Deep.

—WILLIAM SHARP, from *Where the Forest
Murmurs*

1

THE ENCHANTED
WORLD

hat was the enchanted world known to our distant ancestors? My primary goal for this chapter is to provide an understanding of that older view of the world and our part in it. I believe it's important to look at these ideas of the enchanted world and how our ancestors understood things without a reference to science. In our exploration, we will touch upon the various beliefs, practices, and superstitions that formed the magical and metaphysical concepts as they now reside in various forms of Witchcraft. This will lend importance to a variety of components that continue to empower the practice of Witchcraft. I feel that why we believe something is as important as the practical performance connected to it. The reason we do something should empower how we go about performing the work itself.

Everything we now accept as part of Witchcraft had its origins, and if we believe that Witchcraft isn't a modern invention, then those origins must be quite old. I feel it's reasonably certain that Witchcraft evolved into a belief system and practice as opposed to being purposely designed through the imagination of ancient inventors as they sat around the fire at night. I believe it formed as a means of understanding and working with things that seemed magical and mysterious in the world of our ancestors. There was a time when Nature and humankind metaphorically spoke the same language.

Our distant ancestors lived in the deep forests and woodlands. For them, this was not an inhospitable place of wilderness; it was a natural place of dwelling in keeping with the ways of things. Nature is only wild to those who separate themselves from Her. Humans learned to live and survive by embracing the teachings that came directly from existence itself. From a mystical perspective, the spirit of the land communicated with our ancestors (who learned to live in common cause with Nature). From this, humans entered into a relationship with the unseen.

The challenges of survival created social positions within early tribal life. Some people were hunters, gatherers, and warriors, while others built and maintained shelters, made clothing, and prepared food. There were also some members of the tribe who communicated with the unseen world; these people were the forerunners of what we now call Shamans, Seers, Mystics, and Witches. Their role was different within tribal life, and we can say they maintained something akin to a spiritual or religious element within the tribe. When we think of Witchcraft in this light, the question becomes: what was the source and origin of the beliefs in magic and the spirit realm that arose in human culture? Was it invented from the imagination of primitive humans, or was it first experienced by them and then later formed into tenets? Perhaps the most important question is, was it taught to them by sentient beings on the Other Side?

Whatever the process was that led to the beliefs and practices of our ancestors, there isn't a sound reason to believe it's no longer accessible to modern Witches. If beings communicated with humans in ancient times, they can do so today. I believe the key lies in the mind-set of the contemporary Witch. If modern Witches invent, imagine, sense, or envision, then they share something in common with our ancestors. Any ancient belief or practice had its origin and its formation. The enchanted world doesn't originate with one's belief in it or with one's imagination. The enchanted world exists as the inner mechanism, the unseen operation, and this functions no differently now than it did in days of old. It reveals itself to those who do the work to penetrate the inner realms. It further reveals itself to those who are open to receive without resistance or skepticism.

There are very old tales about obstacles and barriers to the Hidden Places. We find this theme in the lore of the oak, ash, and thorn trees. Here we encounter the thorn tree blocking the inner world doorway that's flanked by the oak and ash. Other tales tell of creatures that guard passageways into various secret realms. In some cases, the Hidden Place is surrounded by water and obscured by mist. In order to arrive in any of these secret lands, a quest must be undertaken. Effort is always required, and the doorways never open to those who merely daydream. They remain sealed to those with closed minds, hardened hearts, and doubtful spirits.

Please read the following material thoroughly without skim reading. The concepts are important foundations to understanding the rites, tools, works of magic, and spells in this book. Each piece builds upon another and helps reveal it on a deeper level. Together, all the elements present the enchanted world–view of our ancestors, one that enriches and vitalizes Witchcraft in contemporary practice. You'll miss understanding this if you jump around within this chapter.

FAERIES AND SPIRITS

It seems apparent from anthropological and archaeological studies that our ancestors believed in spirits and various entities that inhabited Nature. Evidence of this appears in tales of beings connected to trees, plants, mountains, rivers, lakes, and oceans. Other beings were believed to dwell in an unseen realm and pass back and forth between this and the world of mortal-kind. One particular race is what humans called the Faery.

Belief in the Faery appears in many lands, and they are depicted in various forms, ranging from tiny winged beings to those who are tall and slender. Among the oldest tales, we find a belief that encounters with Faeries were not always safe or without risk. If we think about first contact with any race, there are possible pros and cons. By analogy, the first white explorers to encounter the tribes of Central and South America came into contact with cultures they didn't understand. The customs, taboos, mind-set, and even the languages were problematic. Some encounters ended in undesirable ways (often for both parties). For further insights, I recommend reading the book *The Secret Commonwealth of Elves, Fauns and Fairies* by Robert Kirk. There are several versions in print by authors such as R. J. Stewart and by John Matthews.

It's my personal belief that Faeries exist in a different dimension than ours (by some accounts the fourth dimension). However, there are passageways that connect to physical places in our own dimension. It's important to understand that Faeries are not human and they don't originate from our world. I believe that as late as the medieval period, Faeries continued to cross over into the world of humankind. We were troublesome and unsettling to them in many ways, and ultimately they withdrew back into their realm of existence. However, sometime around the end of the 19th century, Faeries began to return across the hidden thresholds. Some now work closely with humans who have established the required rapport.

In some discussions about Faeries, the similarities come up between Faery lore and UFO lore. Both tales include floating lights in rural places, odd-looking creatures, kidnapping, time displacement, and a superior technology (in the case of Faeries, this was interpreted by humans as magic). Some people hope for a race of aliens, or Faeries, to come and solve the problems of humanity and to save us in some way. This seems unlikely at best, although helping us to help ourselves is possible. The point I want to make is that it isn't the work of Faeries to do for humans what humans are unwilling or not sufficiently motivated to do for themselves.

Not all systems of Witchcraft have a working connection with Faeries, or even acknowledge them. Instead, what seems more in common among Witchcraft systems and traditions today is embracing the idea of spirits who are native to the earth. Our ancestors knew them as spirits of meadows, forests, rivers, lakes, and mountains. They also knew them as elementals, the spirits of earth, air, fire, and water (the forces of creation and manifestation). These concepts were not invented overnight—they evolved from earlier concepts and the experiences that people had with the Faery.

It's a very ancient idea that spirits exist in Nature and that people have encounters with them. In various forms, they later appear as characters in popular fairytale books. Unfortunately, we lose the deeper elements of these spirits when they're transformed to suit children for entertainment purposes. Additionally, the importance they held for our ancestors becomes lost in tales simply meant to teach a moral or to instill fear as a means of controlling behavior. In order to sort all this out, we must be able to distinguish between folklore and fairytale, and to untangle the comingled threads.

Our ancestors believed not only in spirits of Nature but also in spirits dwelling in unseen realms. The legendary realms of the Underworld and Otherworld likely evolved from this rooted concept. Advanced ideas like the hidden realm of Avalon or the Elysian Fields feature in the constructed tales that originate in past generations. From such tales, we can look deeper in the enchanted world–view of our ancestors.

SACRED DIRECTION AND MYSTICAL THOUGHT

One very old concept appears in the teachings of the seven directions: above, below, in-between, north, east, south, and west. This is still a part of some mystical paths and is highly valued in many of the modern Faery Traditions. The idea symbolizes the points at which we interface with the Universe. It uses the number seven, which has long been regarded in occult circles as representing completion.

I believe that when contemplating the seven directions, the concept of in-between is key and central to the understanding of enchantment. Occult lore instructs us that the in-between places are the most magical. In folkloric traditions, a place such as the threshold of a door is an in-between place. It's neither inside nor outside the door. The crossroads is also often considered to be an in-between place (most commonly the center where the roads meet and divide). Classic stories about Witches depict gathering at the crossroads to perform magic, commune with the dead, and participate in secret rites.

From a mystical perspective, the Material Realm in which we live is envisioned as being in-between. This is because of the ancestral concepts known as above (the celestial) and below (Underworld/ Otherworld) our own world, which means that the mortal world is in-between them. In magical work, we often operate from the concept of us being in the center (sometimes envisioned as a micro-universe). We stand in-between the four directions of a ritual circle: north, east, south, and west. It's in, or through, the in-between places that manifestation comes about. The Material Realm is the place where thoughts become things. There's little magic greater than such a concept.

Through some techniques taught to me by author R. J. Stewart, I had an experience involving an encounter with a Faery who shared with me something of great interest. He described that in the Faery Realm, everything operates within a fluid-like movement (as compared to the Material Realm, where objects appear to remain stationary or keep their formation and place). The Faery gave me an example, saying that when he has a desire to sit, a chair materializes from the fabric of his dimension (what you and I might call energy). When he no longer needs to sit, the chair then withdraws back into the fabric of his realm. The Faery went on to say, *"But humans can create a chair that's there even when they have no need of it. I cannot do that. You are the only beings I know who can make a thought become a thing that's there even when you are not. It's there when you have no need of it, and there even when you are dead."*

The idea of a thought becoming a thing is rooted in the metaphysical principle of manifestation being a process. It's the end result of a directed consciousness (whether it's divine, human, or other). In occult teachings, material objects remain in their form due to what is called an agreement of consciousness. From a scientific perspective, we can say that the atoms and molecules maintain their relationship to one another by some force or energy that keeps a formation cohesive. We can liken this to the idea that planets remain in orbit around a sun. In this light, what the Faery pointed out is that the agreement of consciousness can function uniquely in different dimensions.

If we think about it, our ideas regarding ritual and magic can fall into the category of an agreement of consciousness. For example, we agree about the basic concepts of north, east, south, and west. We further agree that these directions are associated with the four elements of earth, air, fire, and water. Additionally we attach a color to a direction and its associated elemental nature. However, these collected assignments are things that don't actually exist outside of us agreeing they do (and yet we find them functional). In this light, we're working with agreements of consciousness. In this same light, you're able to read this book because you and I share an agreement about the alphabetical letters and the language to which they are assigned. It only functions because we share an agreement.

Returning to the concept of seven directions, we find associated ideas with areas or places. The ancient site of Stonehenge is one example of a physical object tied to directions and to the things associated with them. In this particular example, we find a celestial connection involving the sun, and an earthly connection involving the seasons of our planet. Other sites such as the ancient pyramids of Egypt and their reported alignment to the stars suggest the importance of solidifying agreements of consciousness.

In the tradition of sacred directions, old lore points to what are often called Ley Lines, which is a reference to roads or paths that cross certain geographical areas. These lines crossed directly through ancient sacred sites, and in modern times, they pass through churches built on these formerly Pagan gathering sites. In occult tradition, the Ley Lines are mystical currents of energy flowing through a magical landscape. Various names or titles are associated with the Ley Lines, including the straight tracks, old tracks, and Faery paths. Often the names or titles of these lines begin with the words *black, red,* or *white.* These three colors also appear in many mystery traditions and occult societies. In Chinese lore, the Ley Lines are known as dragon paths. Through all of this, we see that Ley Lines are associated with non-material reality even though they appear as roads in the earthly sense.

Whether we think of the cardinal points of a compass, the concept of three realms (above, in-between, and below), or old Faery paths, we are actually looking at what lies beyond. In other words, the importance is placed on where the direction leads to or what it represents. This always brings us to sacred sites, mystical realms, or things within Nature that are deeply rooted in magic.

SACRED PLACES AND MAGICAL WATER

For countless centuries, people have regarded specific places in special ways. Often something is constructed on such a site that marks its zone or indicates a way into it. From this practice arose the creation of now famous sites from ancient times. Temples were often built on or near these sites, and later on it became the practice to build churches on old sacred sites. The important thing to consider is that this keeps the places active (even though the people who worship there are now followers of the One God who came to displace the Many Gods).

Mircéa Éliade, a historian of religion, wrote in his book *Patterns in Comparative Religion,* that sacred places are not chosen by people—they are discovered by them. In other words, they preexist as sacred places, and at some point they're revealed to people in one way or another. Sacred places are always regarded as separate from the profane or mundane. In this light, for example, a picnic area in a park isn't a sacred spot in comparison to a temple.

The ancient idea of sacred space is linked to the practice of marking it out and sealing it off from other spaces. Sacred space exists due to the forces that first created it, and enclosing it within markers helps to preserve it as well as to draw attention to its precise location. Entering into this place allows a person to share in its source of power and to participate in the sacred process that repeats itself within that sacred space. To stand at its center is to communicate with the source and be vitalized with its essence.

Among the most ancient sites of veneration or worship is the grotto. Into this category we can also place the cave opening. Both of these are commonly associated with water. Most often, this is in the form of water seeping from a crevice or flowing from an inside creek. Within the grotto or cavern, the walls are damp with moisture. This is one of the reasons why caves and grottos came to symbolize the womb, the birthing canal, and the vagina.

Water symbolizes the unformed whole from which the formed part emerges. This represents the idea that water is full potentiality and that anything can emerge from it. In this way, all possibilities exist. Water is also symbolic of renewal, purification, and rebirth. This is because something finite is drawn back into, and is absorbed by, the unlimited. The concept of baptism by water is rooted in this symbolic and mystical idea. A sinner is immersed in water and rises clean of sin because he descends into dissolution and becomes formless, which disconnects him from the former state of sin. Rising back up from the water is a new creation of the individual, a return to the world of formation and a new being within it.

As previously mentioned, the sacred grotto is symbolic of the womb in which we were formed, and the moisture represents its fertile state. In this light, water is the essence of creation. Its presence is always a sign of sacredness. Because water is regarded as cleansing and renewing, it's understood to heal the afflicted. This is one of the reasons why veneration became extended to wells. They tapped into the source of life and to the hidden realm of renewal, full potentiality, and all possibilities. To drop an offering into a sacred well was to plant a seed for manifesting a desire from the limitless realm.

THE MOON AND THE BLACK SACRED NIGHT

The moon was no doubt the greatest mystery to our ancestors because it changed its form monthly, endlessly returning to its original shape again. Yet even its ever-changing nature was predictable. Therefore, it was the constant inconstant light in the night sky. To add to its mystery, the moon seemingly disappeared each month into the blackness of the night sky for three nights. This isn't unlike the idea of seeking renewal through immersion in water.

Black is one of the three colors of the Great Mysteries: Birth, Life, and Death. Like water, black represents the formless state of procreation and the realm of all possibilities. From the ancestral perspective, anything could be lurking in the black of night, and anything might emerge from it. When we factor in that (scientifically speaking) black is the presence of all colors mixed together, we can comprehend the essential nature of its full potentiality. The idea here is that since black contains the all, then any part of that can manifest separately or in combinations.

The moon isn't detached from ideas connected to the concept of blackness. In fact, its cycle of change is well suited for such a mystical realm in which it abides. The color black is often associated with death, and in the writings of ancient Greeks, such as Plutarch, we find a belief that souls of the dead are drawn into the moon. The ancient sect of mystical Pythagoreans also taught a related theme. In occult philosophy, the dead and the moon share the principle of renewed form, which connects to the belief in reincarnation. This suggests an occult mechanism in which the blackness of night represents full potentiality, and the moon symbolizes the means through which the parts of the whole are generated into manifestation. We encountered this fundamental theme in the section on sacred places and magical water.

In the old tales of Witches, the night is the favored time of their gathering, and the preferred place is at a crossroads. We previously noted that the place of the crossroads has long been associated with spirits of the dead, and it's often defined as in-between the worlds. Hecate, one of the classic goddesses associated with Witchcraft, is intimately connected to the dead (and is said to escort them into the Underworld).

The magic of Witches belongs to the night, the moon, and the realms hidden in the black shadowing places. The Full Moon and its rite is the fulfillment of the covenant of the Witch who tends the ancient ways and keeps faith with the tides of the moon. This is because the moon represents the essence of what flows through the mysteries embraced by the Witch. It's enlightenment in the dark places, the cycle of transformation, and the promise of return.

THE GREENWOOD REALM

We know from various sources that our ancestors venerated or worshipped trees. This type of practice must stretch back to something less formalized, perhaps a feeling. Myths and legends are filled with stories of magical forests and enchanted woods. Evolving from ancient practices that are naturally connected to forests are traditions like the Maypole, the Yule log, and what is now called the Christmas tree.

Some of the old tales feature beings attached to trees; the best known are called Dryads. Other stories reveal that gods inhabited trees, and there are tales of gods suspended from trees. One such myth is that of Odin, who hung upside-down from a tree until he gained enlightenment. In mystical Christianity, Jesus is suspended upon a tree in the form of a cross, and this tale is intended to indicate his divine nature. It's an ancient theme in various cultures. All of these themes point to the idea of consciousness associated with trees in one way or another.

Folklorist and poet William Sharp (aka Fiona Macleod) portrayed the consciousness of the forest in one his writings titled "Where the Forest Murmurs." He speaks of becoming aware of something communicating within the forest itself:

> Something is now evident, that was not evident: [it] is entered into the forest. The leaves know it: the bracken knows it: the secret is in every copse, in every thicket, is palpable in every glade, is abroad in every shadow-thridden avenue, is common to the spreading bough and the leaning branch. It is not a rumour; for that might be the wind stealthily lifting his long wings from glade to glade. It's not a whisper; for that might be the secret passage of unquiet airs, furtive heralds of the unloosening thunder. It is not a sigh; for that might be the breath of branch and bough, of fern-frond and grass, obvious in the great suspense. It is an ineffable communication. It comes along the ways of silence; along the ways of sound: its light feet are on sunrays and on shadows. Like dew, one knows not whether it is mysteriously gathered from below or secretly come from on high: simply it is there, above, around, beneath.

Sharp goes on to depict the woodpecker as an agent of the forest that awakens it, keeps it mindful lest the trees fall into slumber. In this light, the woodpecker moves from tree to tree as it senses one withdrawing from its connection to the forest. It then rouses the tree with its hammering beak. Sharp points out that the ancient Italic god Picus (father of the woodland god, Faunus) is associated with the woodpecker. The earliest depiction of Picus shows him as a wooden pillar mounted with a woodpecker. In Ovid's *Metamorphoses*, Book XIV, the Witch Circe is responsible for Picus taking on the form of a woodpecker. This raises the thought that perhaps the Witch is connected to the idea of embracing the forest as something sentient and of maintaining it.

In many old legends, and in a number of fairytales, the Witch lives in the forest or a cabin in the woods. It's the idea of the Witch remaining in the primal world, but not as a rejection of civilization; instead, the Witch chooses to stay connected to the ancestral current that flows from our original home in the forest. There in the deep wooded places, the Witch is one with the Greenwood and its magic. Part of that magic is connected to the vast network of roots that spread beneath the land. Through them, plants tap deeply in to the organic memory of the earth into which the essence of all living things has been absorbed over untold Ages. The Witch, in turn, taps in to the spirit of the plant and calls forth the ancient memories that sleep below.

Who is this Witch of the Greenwood magic? The oldest word in Western Culture to be translated into modern English as "Witch" is the ancient Greek word *Pharmakeute* (pronounced far-mah-koo-tay). Our modern words *pharmacy* and *pharmacist* are derived from the same etymology. In ancient times, most medicine came from plants. The fact that a Witch was first called a Pharmakeute demonstrates the ancient connection between the Witch and plants. In the next chapter, this will be explored in more detail.

In one of the old legends about Witches, we find a special connection with the plant known as vervain. It appears on the charm called the Cimaruta (chee-mah-roo-tah). This is often called the Witches' Charm and is believed by some to be worn as a sign of membership in the ancient society of Witches. Vervain is one of the Faery plants and is associated with the star Sirius. Its blossom has long been a sign of peace when carried by messengers. On the Cimaruta the blossom represents the covenant between the Witch and the Faery Race. This is connected to the idea that Witches are the stewards of the Greenwood in the Material Realm and Fairies are its stewards in the Otherworld. Here we find the concept of the Two Worlds (that of mortal-kind and Faery-kind) along with the idea that they're connected together through a passageway. In folkloric tales, the hollow of a tree is a doorway or portal into the Faery Realm.

The tree as a gateway is an ancient theme. Sometimes the tree is portrayed as a birthing womb. In Virgil's *Aeneid* (Book VIII) the ancient writer states:

These woods were the first seat of sylvan powers,
of nymphs and fauns and savage men who took
their birth from trunks of trees and stubborn oaks.

In the *Odyssey*, the hero is challenged to present his lineage and to distinguish himself from those who "in times of old" were "born of . . . oak or rock." The ancient writer Hesiod states that Zeus made "the brazen race of men" out of ash trees. In Northern Europe, we find the great ash tree known as Yggdrasil, from which all things (including humans) were created.

Historian Mircéa Éliade, in his book *Patterns in Comparative Religion*, writes of the mystical bond between trees and humans. He presents the ancient view that the souls of our ancestors reside in the trees. Éliade also explores the old customs of people marrying trees and the presence of a tree in rites of initiation. The author brings up an interesting concept that humans are "an ephemeral appearance of a new plant modality." He goes on to say that when a human dies, he returns "as a seed" to the tree and enters it in spirit form. In doing so, we become "one with the womb of all things." In this light, "Death is a renewal of contact with the source of all life." Éliade writes of this theme being widespread: "The belief that the souls of ancestors are in some way attached to certain trees from which they pass as embryos into women's wombs form a compact group with a great many variations."

The concept of the tree as a womb-gate or a doorway between the worlds is tied to the theme of the White Tree in Old World Witchcraft. In old folklore, this involves the white birch and spirits of the dead. Early tales of Faery lore in what is now Italy seem to suggest that spirits of the dead could become Faeries. There's some speculation that the concept of Faery mounds evolved from the construction of Neolithic burial mounds, which were made with a single hole in them to allow the soul to enter and exit at will.

The White Tree stands at the in-between place where the material world and the spirit world meet. On the Faery side the tree is a shimmering white light, and on the Mortal side, it's a physical birch tree. From a mystical perspective, Faeries use the White Tree as a doorway to and from the mortal realm. Souls of the dead are said to pass through the tree into the Otherworld. Associated tales portray the Faery World just above the Land of the Dead, suggesting that souls pass through the Faery Realm on their journey.

THE UNDERWORLD

A common theme known to our ancestors is the concept of an afterlife realm that receives the souls of the dead. It was a belief in some cultures that the soul remained in this afterlife realm, while in others the belief held that souls are reborn again into the material world with a new body.

In some old tales, the Underworld (or Otherworld) is located beneath the earth. It has its own sun, moon, and stars. The Underworld is often divided up into different sections, each containing a place of reward or punishment for the souls of the dead. Over the course of time, stories arose in which the living could journey to the Underworld. In some tales, the traveler needed to carry a magical object such as the silver bough or golden bough with her or him, which granted safe passage to and from the Land of the Dead. In Northern European lore, the silver bough is a magical branch given by the Queen of the Faeries. In Southern European lore, the golden bough is a magical branch that must be sought out and obtained in the hero's quest.

Water is often included in tales of the Underworld/Otherworld, and we have seen reasons for its functional inclusion. In Greek mythology, there are rivers in the Underworld, and in the legends of Northern Europe, we find islands in mystical lakes to which the dead journey. Considering occult beliefs associated with water, there's little wonder why rivers, lakes, and wells appear in tales of the dead.

The role of water as something that both absorbs and renews is vital to our understanding.

One universal idea is that the newly dead arrive in the Land of the Dead with great thirst. As a result, they seek to cool their thirst at the springs of the Underworld. In the mystery tradition, we find mention of two springs or wells. One contains the water of memory and the other the water of forgetfulness. Sometimes they are located at the crossroads in the Underworld where the soul must choose to drink from one or the other.

Greek historian Professor Margaret Alexiou, in her book *The Ritual Lament in Greek Tradition,* writes of souls and the waters of the Underworld. She describes the tears of the living as flowing down into the Underworld to "greet" the dead. These tears are so bountiful that they form a river or lake through which the dead can be reached. Professor Alexiou quotes an unnamed ancient text addressing mourners that reads:

Why do you stand there, orphaned children, like strangers, like passers-by?...
Why do your eyes not run like a quiet river,
so that your tears become a lake and make a cool spring,
for the unwashed to be washed, for the thirsty ones to drink?

Alexiou goes on to say that it's this river, lake, or spring that makes contact possible between the living and the dead.

In this chapter, we have looked at the many beliefs that are foundational to popular concepts found in modern Witchcraft. Although the generational interpretations and representations of them have somewhat altered them, the core teachings still make them vital and carry them through time. In the next chapter, we will examine how such concepts appear and function within what is today called Old World Witchery.

2

THE ROSE AND
THORN PATH

The Path of Witchcraft remained secret for many centuries. It was shrouded in mystery, legend, superstition, and the supernatural. Here it largely remained until the writings of two key authors. The first was Charles Leland, and the second was Gerald Gardner. These men presented Witchcraft as a contemporary practice during their lifetimes. Leland wrote in the late 19th century, and Gardner in the mid-20th century. Authors in earlier periods certainly wrote about the practice of Witchcraft, but Leland and Gardner were the first to claim knowledge of Witchcraft practices from people actively involved in them (and who claimed an ancient lineage). Although there's much debate concerning the authenticity of what they presented, their writings opened the way to shed some public light on the practice of Witchcraft. The value here is that the voices of people calling themselves Witches (without coercion) became added to the voices of non-Witches who likely never even met a Witch (by any definition). The beliefs and perspectives of the latter formed the so-called official history of Witchcraft touted by academics, which many people accept to be the truth despite the unreliable witnesses.

Since the writings of these two authors, many systems and traditions of Witchcraft became well-known, as did their founders or lineage bearers. They vary from claims of antiquity to traditional to entirely modern. One of the lesser-known systems is what its practitioners refer to as Old Word Witchery. It differs in key ways from Traditional Witchcraft, as you will see as this chapter unfolds the practitioner's view.

The primary current of Old World Witchery is known as the Path of the Rose and Thorn. The core elements of this system also appear in a variety of Witchcraft traditions and systems (even those not based upon its composition). It should be noted that the Rose and Thorn Path doesn't identify itself as Traditional Witchcraft or as an offshoot. People claiming the label Traditional Witchcraft define it in such a way that the Rose and Thorn Path doesn't meet the constraints of qualification. However, the similarities are striking nonetheless. The primary difference is that the mythos of the Rose and Thorn Path doesn't contain lore associated with Lilith, Cain, or anything related to the culture from which such elements seemingly originated. It's also not solely a practice of sorcery but is almost something that one could call a religion of the Old Greenwood.

In Old World Witchery, thorns represent protection and boundary as well as initiation and enlightenment. They are the challenges that lead to attainment, and thorns are also symbols of acknowledgment for earned achievements. In the Rose and Thorn Path, the long-stemmed rose represents a ladder (the rows of thorns) leading to enlightenment and attainment (the blossom). Other types of thorns appear as well in the symbolism of this system.

In this system, there are three primary thorns: blackthorn, hawthorn, and the rose thorn. These appear as the tips on the Trident of the Inner Mysteries, which symbolizes the empowered quest of the true seeker. It's the crossroads, the depths, the heights, and the lightning flash of realization. To wield the trident is to master the elements of one's own nature and character, which have been purified by the Way of the Thorn Path. In this light, the trident symbolizes the self in the center flanked by the duality of transformative forces. See chapter 8, "The Old Rites," for details about using the trident.

The hawthorn guards the mysteries from casual access, the black-thorn challenges the seeker's dedication, and the rose reveals the portal that opens into the center of all things. This center is symbolized by the rose blossom. Later in this chapter, we'll explore the vital concepts known as the Thorn Gate and the Gathered Thorns. These present important teachings about personal power and the spirit of the Witch.

Thorns, as symbols of protection, are often associated with the legendary Faery thicket. Several ideas are attached to the theme of this thicket. One idea depicts the Faery thicket as a magical barrier protecting the Faery Realm from being entered by ill-prepared or unworthy explorers. This barrier presents itself as a tangled border of vines and gnarled branches covered with a myriad of menacing thorns. This keeps out the idle curious, and it invites the stout hearted to a significant challenge.

A Faery thicket can also be thought of as a type of maze in which the unwary become entrapped. Some people regard this in the mental sense of becoming lost and confused, which is also known as being Faery led into entanglement. Here we encounter the teaching that the Mysteries are not readily open to anyone simply for the asking. This is an unpopular concept in modern times but one that's time-proven nonetheless. That being said, no mystery is ever closed to an open mind.

Thorns as symbols of challenge appear in tales of transformation and are often markers of endurance or sacrifice in order to achieve transformation. This theme even appears in mystical forms of Christianity as the crown of thorns worn by the Christ figure. His death on a tree (wooden cross) connects him to the plant kingdom and identifies him as a sacrificial Lord of the Harvest. This symbolism is intimately connected to the Greenwood Realm, which is an integral part of Old World Witchery. Watered-down versions of the Harvest Lord appear in contemporary Wiccan and Neo-Pagan ritual themes in order to make them more palatable. Connected to the old theme within the Rose and Thorn Path is the Covenant of the Blood. This involves a ritual exchange of three drops of human blood (upon the crown of a rose bush) for three drops of green blood (liquid chlorophyll) taken orally. More details are given later in this book.

The theme of the thorn in association with enlightenment or attainment isn't a common one. Most people may think that a thorn is always a deterrent. However, in Old World Witchery, the rose thorn penetrates into the inner mysteries. In this context, it represents the catalyst, the initiating moment, and the process leading to altered states of consciousness. The act of pricking by thorn can cause what is called blood poisoning. For the Witch of the Thorn Path, this is viewed through metaphors, and in this light, the Witch is the Pharmaceute—the alchemical botanist of the Green Realm; but more importantly, the Witch is the Seer of the mystical spirit behind manifestation.

Witchcraft was once called *veneficium,* a term that scholars define as "Witchcraft." In this same regard, a Witch was called a *venefica* (literally a "poisoner"). Poisoning through the magical arts was known as *veneficus.* What is ignored, however, is the fact that the root Latin word *vene* is derived from *Venus.* The goddess Venus was originally a deity of cultivated gardens before she became the goddess of love (see chapter 4, "Plant Spirits of the Greenwood"). It was the making of love potions from herbs, and the accusation that love potions poisoned the will of its target, that erroneously stained the Witch as one who literally poisons others to death through her arts. In the public arena, everything about the Art of Witchcraft was then interpreted and portrayed in this erroneous context.

In shamanic traditions, we sometimes find the use of venom as a means of contacting powerful spirits. One example, found in some American Indian traditions, is the ritual act of allowing a rattlesnake to bite the ritual participant. The resulting intoxication alters the consciousness, which opens the person to inner levels of communication with nonmaterial reality. This is an extremely dangerous and potentially lethal method that I strongly discourage readers from ever attempting. It's safer to work with spirits than it is to allow toxins into your body. Chapter 4 will offer you this as a viable and powerful alternative.

Initiation into the Rose and Thorn Path is, in its practical phase, one of spirit contact. At its core, it's a Green Realm experience, an entering into the mystical essence of plant spirits. There are two levels connected to the experience of initiation and the transformation that takes place as a result. The first concept is that of the organic memory of the earth, and the second is union with a specific plant entity who holds the key to interfacing with the unseen. This being is called She of the Thorn-Blooded Rose, and more about her will follow in chapter 4.

The teachings of the Rose and Thorn Path are centered in the concept of the descended-star knowledge and its role in the soul's journey through Material Realm existence. This is rooted in the legend of a star entity named Kaelifera, who descends and penetrates the earth, entering deep into its mystical core. This mythos sets the preface for what is called the Thorn Gate teachings, which is a related teaching connecting the theme of the star-being with the soul of the Witch. It's a type of "as above, so below" philosophy that reflects the higher and lower nature. Herein we see the journey of the soul as a parallel to the mythos of the descended star entity that also moves from the celestial to the terrestrial (and back again).

The Thorn Gate concept envisions the soul as having descended from the stellar realm, which is a metaphor for the Otherworld (known by many other names). As the soul moves toward reincarnation, it's imprinted with a solar emanation and takes on a specific resonance. In occult philosophy, this imprint is the Sun Sign as understood through the natal chart. In effect, this is a spiritual map or blueprint that's available to the soul in any given incarnation. In each lifetime, it serves to provide the soul with a separate persona through which to experience and work within each incarnation. By analogy, this isn't unlike an actor becoming and animating a character within a movie.

As the process of reincarnation proceeds, the soul passes through a lunar emanation in which it's enveloped in an astral form, or body, which will then become its flesh counterpart once it enters the Material Realm. In mortal form, the soul is connected to the Spirit of the Land, and through this the soul can reunite with the organic memory of the earth. In the Rose and Thorn Path, this is called Shadow, which is the accumulated knowledge of all living things that died and were absorbed into the earth. The spoken affirmation of the Thorn-Blooded Witch arises with these words:

"I am a Thorn-Blooded Witch of the Old Ways.
I am descended from the stars,
Fated by the sun,
Envisioned by the moon,
Given form by the land,
And I stand with feet rooted in Shadow,
And reach upward to the stars."

Among the old beliefs preserved in the Rose and Thorn Path teachings is the idea of lasting memory, and this is tied into the initiation by thorn. Stories persist through time about Witch blood and its importance within families possessing such a lineage. One belief is that the Witch grows in power each time she or he reincarnates in the same family bloodline. In some Witch lore is the belief that Witch blood is the result of mating between mortals and Faeries. Whatever the case may be, the blooded thorn holds particular value and inner meaning for initiates of the Rose and Thorn Path.

A bold concept exists that's known as the living river of blood, which reflects the belief in a surviving element of ancestral memory. The belief is that our DNA conveys or transmits more than just the instructions on how to build us; it also carries an energy imprint that connects us to all in our bloodline who passed their DNA on to future generations. In this light, we are all the present stewards of the living river of blood that flows from the generation to generation. But we are not alone in the memory chain, for there's another component, which is the principle of Shadow. Earlier I referred to this as the organic memory of the earth (an earthly equivalent to the notion of the Akashic Records in metaphysical philosophy originating from Eastern mysticism).

Beneath the surface of the land lies the bone memory of all living things that died and were absorbed into the earth. Memory is retained in the mineral composition, and plants absorb minerals through their roots. This makes them vessels through which Shadow can be tapped and used by the Witch. In the Rose and Thorn Path, plant spirits are evoked in order to communicate with Shadow. The collective memory of all Witches who came before us resides in Shadow and is a vast source upon which to draw from the ancestors. It's through an established rapport with plant spirits that this becomes accessible to the Witch.

One phase of the initiation rite involves establishing an intimate link with the previously mentioned spirit called She of the Thorn-Blooded Rose. This entity serves as a go-between for mortals and plant spirits and is a powerful ally within the Green Realm. At one point in the initiation process, the initiate offers three drops of her or his blood from a pricking by a rose thorn. This is mixed with water and poured out on the base of a dedicated rose bush. The initiate then drinks a sip of the green blood (liquid chlorophyll) in a ritual exchange of life fluids. Through this, the Witch and She of the Thorn-Blooded Rose join in a relationship that opens portals to the Greenwood Magic and to the hidden Realm of Shadow.

Among the means of connecting with Shadow is the use of what is called the Well of the Moon. It's envisioned as an old stone well with twenty-seven stones forming the ledge and encircling the dark pool of water below. When viewed from above, it takes on the appearance of a dragon's eye. The water in the well is a deep black color that doesn't reflect any image above it. It's the portal directly into Shadow, and through mystical methods the Witch must enter into the black water and descend into the core of the organic memory of the earth. This technique is provided in chapter 8, "The Old Rites."

In the Rose and Thorn Path, the ability to work effectively with the Green Realm and to use techniques involving Shadow and the Well of the Moon is derived from a specific training known as the Gathered Thorns. It's composed of five levels of training: herbalism, magic, spirit mediumship, mysticism, and seership. Each is symbolically represented by one of five red thorns encircling a black pentagon figure. The thorn itself, as a symbol, signifies the challenges and efforts involved in mastering each facet of training. The central black pentagon figure symbolizes Shadow, and the thorns are the blood links to it, which is why each thorn is colored red in the Thorn Path imagery of the Gathered Thorns design. To gather a thorn is to complete a phase of training.

The thorn symbol represents several concepts within the Thorn Path system of Witchcraft. Thorny thickets are often regarded as protections, and in some tales, they are guardians and barriers that guard mystical doorways or passages. This theme is essential in the approach to the inner mysteries and how the way is made open. Witchcraft isn't, in the view of the Rose and Thorn Path, a practice that simply involves spells, recipes, and methods. It's instead a realization of the mystical web that connects all things and the Witch's place and role in it all. It's the enchanted world–view of our ancestors, which is kept alive and adapted to practical needs of contemporary life. This isn't, however, done to the degree that sacrifices the time-proven and time-honored Ways of Witchcraft in favor of modern trends and politics.

The ancient Greek idea of the Witch as the Pharmakeute represents a spiritual tradition (even though not historically presented as such). In ancient times, intoxication was believed to be possession by the spirit of the plant, and one example of this is found in the rites of Dionysus. The god of the vine entered into the worshipper as she or he drank the sacred wine, and the internal presence of the god caused a state of ecstasy. This ancient theme appears in the Christian communion rite of consuming wine and wafers, although in this case the belief is one of attaching the soul to the resurrection of the slain god (as opposed to the concept of internal possession itself).

In the Rose and Thorn Path, the focus is on a spiritual botany as opposed to the common idea of the Witch as an herbalist. The practices are more of an etheric alchemy than they are the practice of a Witch as a material herbalist. Physical plants are certainly used in the system, but they are viewed as connections and conduits to nonmaterial reality and the beings within it that are reachable through the portal of the material plant realm. What is sought is contact and communication with the chthonic spirits that are attached to specific plants, particularly the traditional plants associated with Witchcraft. But these spirits do not readily make themselves available, nor are they naturally predisposed to a benevolent relationship with humankind.

To gain a reliable, and therefore practical, rapport with plant spirits, it's advisable to begin with She of the Thorn-Blooded Rose who will in turn introduce the seeker to the Mandrake Spirit. The mandrake is the natural conduit between humans and the Green Realm, and it demonstrates this nature by forming its root to resemble human shape. Its power in the Green Realm has earned the mandrake the title of the Sorcerer's Root. To bear such a root keeps the Witch in the stream of the Greenwood Magic (and all that it reaches).

The Witch of the Rose and Thorn Path carries a small pouch bearing the rose thorn of initiation, a pinch of soil from a crossroads, a small portion of cemetery dust (finely ground bark from a tree in the center of a cemetery), and a piece of mandrake root. To this may be added other selected items of witchery for personal empowerment. All of these help to maintain a connection to the ancestral current through the blood and through the places intimately linked to the dead. The consciousness of specific places and the link to blood lineage merge into one important element of the Rose and Thorn Path. This involves the tending of the Shadow Garden in which the plants of the Witches' Craft are grown and empowered.

A Shadow Garden contains the plants used in magic and ritual. It's valued not only for the connective roots that move down into the organic memory of the earth but also as a place where ritual debris is buried. The latter involves the concept of passing the memory of each rite into the soil where, in turn, the plants absorb this through their roots. In this way, the ancient memories contained in Shadow are blended with the memory of each contemporary rite. The plants then become vessels for the quintessence of rituals (adding what is new to what is ancient). This builds a sturdy bridge between past and present practitioners of the Witchcraft, and through this a spiritual lineage is born by practitioners in the living generation.

Every Shadow Garden contains a dedicated rose bush, and this becomes the interfacing point for communing with She of the Thorn-Blooded Rose. It also connects with the theme of the Witch as the Pharmakeute, which in turn links to the archaic plant nature of the goddess Venus, who is also known as the Lady of the Rose. The physical plants are under her care and domain, while the spirits of the plants belong to She of the Thorn-Blooded Rose. Within the Shadow Garden, plants are grouped into divisions, and each sector is assigned a subject matter such as love, prosperity, protection, success, or health. Plants corresponding to these matters are placed in the appropriate section of the garden. The debris from a spell or ritual is worked into the area of the Shadow Garden in accordance with its nature. In other words, debris from a prosperity spell goes into the prosperity section of the garden and so on. This adds magical power from the performance of spells and rituals to the plants growing in each section. Make sure not to put toxic debris in the garden soil.

Another element of the Shadow Garden is the idea of the thorn blood connection to the Spirit of the Land, and to the Greenwood Realm itself. The blood that's offered to the land establishes a covenant between Witch and Shadow. The life essence of blood from the living passes into the organic memory of the earth. This links the Witch to all of his kind who came before and whose memories reside in the bone memory of the earth (the mineral composition). The blood freely offered by the Witch becomes a connective nerve through which Shadow can be aroused. In turn, the act connects the

Witch with the Spirit of the Land and the many spirits that dwell in the area. The Witch becomes known through all that the blood can reveal. When embraced by all these spirits and entities, the Witch then becomes a knower, and the circle is completed.

When blood is mixed with some water and poured out on the crown of a plant (which is just above the roots), a covenant is established between the Witch and the spirit of the plant. This also makes the Witch kindred to the spirit, which opens the way for communication. A type of blood brother exchange (red and green) takes place between human and plant. From this is formed the blood kin relationship. The result helps to create a rapport and a trust between both. This covenant is vital for the Witch to be the Pharmakeute in the eyes of the plant spirits. A vervain blossom is the special symbol of the old covenant.

In the Ways of the Rose and Thorn Path, thorns penetrate into the inner places, but the rose teaches that thorns can also be ladders to enlightenment. This is why the Thorn Path symbol of the Mystery Rose depicts rungs of thorns along the stem leading to the blossom. To reach for the blossom, and in the process be pierced by thorns, is to be transformed in mind, body, and spirit.

STEPPING STONES ALONG THE THORN PATH

There are five envisioned realms associated with the metaphorical thorns of Old World Witchery. Each is considered to be a force that imprints its nature on anything coming into contact with it. These points of contact are thought of as dimensions or zones. The tips of a five-pointed star mark each of these in a specific order:

1. Celestial

2. Solar

3. Lunar (Astral)

4. Material (Spirit of the Land)

5. Shadow (the organic memory of the earth)

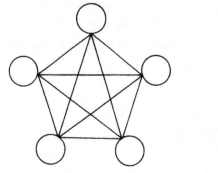 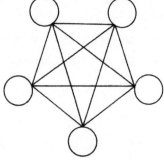

The five-pointed star is composed of five thorn tips, which on the glyph are colored red to represent blooded thorns. The center pentagon shape is colored black, the color of full potentiality and the state of procreation. The Thorn-Blooded Witch aligns with symbolic concepts by touching each tip of the star. This is done in conjunction with the proclamation related to each point and the realm it represents. Let's explore four key realms before examining the five points of the star that share a relationship.

The Celestial Realm is thought of as a dimension of light beings that includes souls who are unattached to physical bodies. This philosophy is rooted in the occult idea of Four Worlds: Material, Lunar, Solar, and Stellar. In such teachings, the soul evolves by experiencing existence in all Four Worlds. It begins with the creation of the soul in the Stellar World and its first vessel (body) in the Material World. It evolves through a series of lives in bodies of flesh, and once liberated from the cycle of rebirth within the material dimension, the soul moves to its next cycle in the Lunar World. In this world, it takes on a moon body and experiences existence in this world. This continues next to existence in the Solar, and then finally the soul returns to the Stellar World, where it resides in the Community of Souls.

The Material World is a dimension in which energy vibrates at an extremely low frequency (so slowly that things appear to be dense and cohesive). Slightly higher in vibration is the Lunar World (where things have distinct forms but are less dense and can alter shape). The Solar World is a dimension in which things have no stationary form and are always in motion (much like the flames in a hearth or bonfire). The Celestial World is a dimension of pure light where consciousness can manifest any of the properties and natures of the other dimension. It's the one dimension that's not dependent upon energy to maintain it.

In viewing the five thorns on the star symbol, we have the placement of Shadow on the lower left tip. Shadow is the organic memory of the earth, which contains all that has decomposed into the land. It lies beneath our feet and is directly tapped by the roots of trees and plants. Mineral formations hold the bone memory of the earth and have their place in Old World Witchery (discussed further in other chapters).

THE GATE OF THORNS: FIVE POINTS OF ESOTERIC TEACHING

As previously described, the Gate of Thorns depicts the journey of the soul through reincarnation. In this teaching, the soul's natural realm is Celestial; it's star born (and is naturally at home in the Community of Souls that reside outside of material reality). When a soul needs to return to the experience of material reality, it withdraws from its realm. This is referred to as the descent. This action is symbolically marked by the upper tip of a five-pointed star, and is affirmed in the first of the six proclamations made by the Thorn-Blooded Witch: "*I am descended from the stars.*" Such an affirmation keeps us connected to our higher nature as celestial beings. This is important so that we do not lose ourselves within the constrained reality and the experience of a physical body with a conscious personality. The soul and the personality share consciousness but are not one and the same.

In each incarnation, the soul takes on a distinct personality that it wears in each lifetime. You can think of this in the following way. In this current lifetime, you were once six years old, and then additional ages until reaching whatever age you are now. At each age, you looked different, experienced life differently, did certain things, and had interests appropriate to each period in your life. You are no longer the person at each age you once were, although you do carry the individual memories. As you grow up, each "personality" is left behind, but from all of them you possess an accumulation of their experiences and knowledge. In this same way, the soul isn't any single personality through which it operated in any given reincarnation. Instead it's one being who grows and evolves through extensions of itself as people in various lives. It's who you truly are, and your distinct personality in this life is like an actor performing in a movie (the actor must become the character she's playing in order for the role to be believable). However, when the movie is completed, the actor returns to functioning as her true self (by analogy, the soul reemerging from the personality at death).

A soul evolves from its experiences in material reality, for in this realm the finite and the linear are encountered. These are states that are quite different from the limitless and conceptual realities that are natural to the soul. Through immersion into material reality, the soul learns to apply its consciousness rather than simply be consciousness. In other words, through integrating an understanding of how things become manifest, the soul comes to a fuller appreciation and comprehension of the Whole (and the parts that created it).

In the material plane, thoughts become things, meaning that ideas become tangible objects. By analogy, this book you are holding was previously just an idea I had, a project that I envisioned. Now it's a material object (or in the case of an ebook, it's manifesting through an object—the reading device). My thoughts became a thing, but this can only take place in material reality. On the soul plane, it would simply be a concept without its parts. Metaphorically speaking, the process, the parts, and the end results are the education of the soul on the material plane. In this light, we can say that the soul experiences physical lives through which it learns the lessons only material reality can teach.

Continuing with the Thorn Gate Thorn elements, the second tip of the five-pointed star symbolizes the passage of the soul descending through the Solar Realm. This aspect brings into play the idea that in each reincarnation, the personality is influenced by the astrological Sun Sign at the time of physical birth. A natal chart becomes the blueprint design for the personality in any given lifetime journey. The second tip of the star is linked to the Witch's proclamation: "*I am fated by the Sun.*" In this light, there's the perception of an element of Fate attached to the soul in any given lifetime, but this isn't Fate in the sense of something inescapable. Instead, this is viewed as the design or pattern first woven. But personal free will can alter the original course, as can the actions of others who likewise have free will at their command. It's part of the answer as to why bad things happen to good people.

The third thorn symbolizes the soul descending through the Astral World and at this point, the tip of the star calls for the proclamation: "*I am envisioned by the moon.*" This is tied to the idea that the astral substance forms around anything that enters it, and you can think of this like someone putting his hand in melted wax. The liquid wax coats the hand and essentially creates a replica of it. In this action, the melted wax becomes solid. In this light, the soul can be thought of as being wrapped in an astral coating. This creates an astral form, and in occult philosophy, it's taught that astral forms move toward manifestation on the material plane. This is because once they solidify on the Astral Realm, they are no longer compatible there because their original nature is changed. The density and nature of the astral substance is transformed when it forms around something. Therefore, astral forms sink down into the Material World because they are closer in nature to it after becoming a solidified astral form. In occult philosophy, the term is *like attracts like.*

The fourth tip of the star signifies the Material World and here the proclamation is *"I am given form by the Land."* This statement affirms that the astral body is integrated into one of flesh as it's drawn into material reality. This is a type of "as above, so below" philosophy, meaning that just as the astral substance formed around the soul, so too does a body of flesh encase it.

The idea of the land goes beyond a term for the physical plane. Its deeper meaning reflects a belief that consciousness exists within matter. The Spirit of the Land is an old concept and is tied into the idea of the *genii loci* (a term for spirits that abide in special areas or regions). The philosophy of the Rose and Thorn Path is that a Witch returns in each life to connect with spirits and entities known to it in a previous life. This need not be specific to a place. It's more often a matter of reconnecting with certain types of spirits. Through this, the Witch is rejoined to guides and allies that aided it in other lifetimes. The old alliances are time-proven in their power and endurance.

The fifth tip of the star represents the concept of Shadow and is marked by the proclamation: *"I stand with feet rooted in Shadow."* This refers to the Witch's connection to the organic memory of the earth. Here lie the memories of all that transpired outside of the personal experience of the Witch in any given lifetime. This isn't unlike the concept of the Akashic Records, a teaching originating in Eastern Mysticism. However, the idea of Shadow is something very primal in origin, which nicely suits the nature of European Witchcraft and best connects with its spiritual lineage.

When we think about Shadow, the mind and spirit are drawn to visions of ancient places. The ancient forests have fallen and been absorbed into Shadow, as have all the ancient practitioners of magic, ritual, and mysticism. Their memories reside in the Cavern of the Ancestors, which is an occult concept for a realm of consciousness wherein the living and the dead can meet (as well as past and present, in general, sharing one space and time together). In the belief system of the Rose and Thorn Path, ancient standing stones and the ruins of temples mark zones of access used long ago by generations of the past. They remain as beacons for those who understand the principles.

The five-pointed star symbolism is completed by a return to the uppermost tip. Here, the proclamation becomes *"I reach upward to the stars."* This refers to the concept that the soul returns to the celestial and ultimately joins the Community of Souls in the metaphorical Celestial World. Through this ongoing alignment, the soul maintains the etheric thread through which its higher nature is secured.

THE GATHERED THORNS, ROOTS OF POWER

When the five-pointed star is set with two tips facing upward, it represents the five powers of the Witch. These powers arise from training and experience in the time-honored arts of Witchcraft. Such arts may differ from system to system, but in the Rose and Thorn Path, they are herbalism, magic, spirit mediumship, mysticism, and seership.

The first art is that of herbalism, and appears on the five-pointed star as the lower left side tip that faces down. The Witch as a Pharmakuete is foundational in Old World Witchery. This title speaks to possessing special knowledge of plant substances, but more importantly, it indicates an intimate rapport with plant spirits. Through both, the Witch is able to exert influence within material and non-material reality. The proclamation associated with this tip is *"I am the knower of plants."*

In the Thorn Path, plants are a direct connection to the forces that sustain the Greenwood Realm. Through them, the forces of birth, life, death, and renewal flow into the Witch and link her/him to the inner mechanism. This is reflected in part of the Witch's chant: *"From seed to sprout, sprout to leaf, leaf to bud, bud to flower, flower to seed."* Such words bring the generative forces of Nature into the hands of the Witch.

The second point of focus on the five-pointed star is the upper right hand tip, which signifies divination. This is the Witch as the Seer, one who can perceive patterns forming in the Astral World which in turn can become realities in the Material World. The proclamation at this tip is *"I am the Seer of all that approaches."* Some people refer to this as the ability to predict future events, the gift of oracle. However, the idea in the Rose and Thorn Path is that the future isn't set in stone. The future is potentiality and probability. The Witch looks into the patterns that are taking shape, much like a meteorologist looks at weather patterns to predict the weather. When the Witch predicts the future, she or he is essentially saying that if prevailing patterns go unchanged, then such and such is most likely to occur. The gift of divination lies in the ability to see what is coming, which then allows the person to alter the predicted future outcome or prepare for its arrival.

The third symbolic tip of the five-pointed star appears at the bottom where the single tip faces downward. This represents the Witch as a type of Spirit Medium, one who communicates with spirits of the dead. The proclamation at the third tip is *"I am the hearer of the whispering dead."* In the Rose and Thorn Path, spirits of the dead are honored and remembered in both heart and ritual. There's no true severance between the living and the dead; through ritual, both join together during the night of the Full Moon. In a much larger view of the dead, we embrace the concept of the Ancestral Spirit. This can be thought of as the collective consciousness of all who came before us. It's the gateway to a lineage (whether genetic or spiritual).

One primitive way of thinking about the dead is that they have gone to a place where we will one day follow. They are farther up the road, so to speak, and can look back and see us journeying behind them. You can think of this like hikers following guides who have passed out of sight around the side of a hill. When we call out to them, they can offer advice about what you have yet to encounter as you continue to climb the hill. In this light, the dead can be thought of as oracle spirits. But more importantly, they have a vested interest in our survival among the living, for we are the Keepers of the Living River of Blood in the current generation (as discussed in chapter 1). Our survival is a stepping-stone to their continuation through to future generations.

The fourth tip of the five-pointed star is symbolically placed at the upper left-hand side where it faces upward. This represents the Witch as the Mystic, one who sees past form and into what lies behind it. The proclamation associated with the fourth tip is *"I am born of this world, but am not of this realm."* The Mystic understands that material reality is a perception through which people experience their lives. For example, we know from science that material objects are a collection of atoms, molecules, and electrons. There's space between them all within their patterned formation, and therefore the object isn't actually solid. However, it appears to be solid and we experience it as solid, but it isn't. So what is it? It's cohesive, not solid. In other words, the atoms, molecules, and electrons maintain their pattern and relationship to one another, which results in what we perceive as a specific material object.

The Mystic perceives different levels of reality and operates in a Universe containing material reality and nonmaterial reality. One way of thinking about this is to look at what we call the conscious mind and the subconscious mind. Each of them deals with perceptions of reality. The conscious mind deals with things that appear finite and linear. The subconscious mind deals with things that appear unlimited and conceptual. The Mystic understands that each mind is half of our consciousness. The conscious mind isn't us—it's only half of our awareness. In this light, it's odd that people allow it to direct their lives, which if you think about it, is a half-witted approach.

The subconscious mind is equally not us but is half of our consciousness. It's at home in the so-called dream world where anything is possible. People don't think of this consciousness as being them (at least not in the same way as they do the conscious mind). Instead, they tend to regard it as the generator of dreams and the brooder of personal issues that influence emotions and behavior. People appear to believe that they experience the subconscious rather than it being half of the total mind they possess and through which they must operate as sentient animated beings. In other words, they regard the subconscious mind as a program running in the conscious mind (instead of it being a distinct mind of its own).

The Witch, as a Mystic, joins the conscious and subconscious minds together into a single mind that's not dominated by either one. It's not a third consciousness; it's an undivided one working as a single unit at all times. Through this, we do not separate reality into dreaming the impossible or keeping with the constraints of the waking world. Instead, we seek the fullness of both through the fusion of consciousness. In doing so, we bring the limitless into the realm of limits, transformation into that which is cohesive, and complete possibility into that which is constrained by probability. This is discussed in more detail in my book *Old World Witchcraft*.

It's the mystical nature of the Witch that empowers her/him with the means to actualize the concept of magic and to live it each day. In this light, the Witch doesn't believe—instead she/he knows. The Witch doesn't possess faith—she/he possesses realization. This comes about because the Witch doesn't limit her or his perception to one realm of existence or one stream of consciousness.

The fifth tip of the five-pointed star is found on the lower right-hand side of the figure. It marks the Witch as a user of magic. The proclamation of the fifth tip is *"I wield the forces that move all tides and seasons."* The intimate connection to the energy of magic comes from the mentality of the Witch as a mystic. Magic is the ability to use a force or stream of consciousness to manifest personal will, intent, or desire. It arises when objections to its reality are displaced or dissolved away.

Magic is what most often first comes to mind when people think about Witchcraft. However, in the Rose and Thorn Path, it's the fifth aspect in the Witch's training. The other tips of the five-pointed star reveal that magical training is best undertaken in conjunction with an understanding of Witchcraft as a whole. The intentional application of magic is always last, for the Witch has at her/his service the Gathered Thorns of the Witch's nature. These keys are often enough to live a gainful and satisfying life without evoking or invoking a directed change or alteration through magic.

In this chapter, we have explored the mystical elements found within the practice of Old World Witchery. The Witch, however, must also be well-grounded in the earthly realm. The hands-on aspect of practicing Witchcraft is most commonly observed in the use of magical and ritual tools. Let us turn now to the next chapter and take up the tools of the Witches' Craft.

3

TOOLS OF THE WITCHES' CRAFT

The use of various tools in the practice of Witchcraft, whether ancient or modern, isn't a new concept. Ancient literature depicts Witches such as Medea using a wand, a dagger, and a cauldron. In many forms of modern Witchcraft, we find the well-known grouping of a pentacle, a wand, a dagger, and a chalice. These classic tools are known as the Four Ritual Tools of Western Occultism and are also associated with the suit cards in classic Tarot symbolism. In the ancient cult of the Mithras, we find the use of a platter, a wand, a dagger, a cup, a sword, and a whip. These bring to mind the ritual tools of Gardnerian Witchcraft/Wicca.

From time to time, people tell me they don't need tools in order to work magic or perform rituals. I agree that eventually the Witch arrives at a point where tools are no longer necessary, although they are essential in the early stages of training (more on that later). While I admit that tools are ultimately unnecessary, I always add the following point to the discussion. I can eat a plate of spaghetti without a fork by simply shoving my face down onto the plate and slurping up the noodles. However, using utensils (tools) makes it quite a different experience overall. Yet, with or without the tools, the end result is the same.

One important element to be considered when we talk about tools is the idea of sacredness. The typical dictionary definition of *sacred* is "something dedicated to or set apart for the worship of divinity." It can also be regarded as worthy for use in the veneration of a deity. In the Rose and Thorn Path, we define sacred as something dedicated to a single use or purpose in the Witches' Craft. It does not require a connection to anything commonly regarded as religious in nature.

The primary tool of Old World Witchery is the mortar and pestle set. It's an essential tool when working with Greenwood Magic. The mortar represents the womb gate, the source through which things manifest in the material world. By extension, it can be thought of as the earth envisioned as a cauldron that generates life and draws it back in to itself again. For those who seek a religious or spiritual connotation, the mortar can represent the womb of the Great Mother Goddess. However, the Great Mother concept isn't an official part of any formal pantheon in the Rose and Thorn Path.

As a ritual and magical tool, the mortar is called Life Giver as well as Death Taker. It connects with the former nature through which it can be used to generate and to reanimate. For the latter, it's used to terminate and to decompose. This is detailed in chapter 5, "Works of Magic." For now, you can simply be aware of the dual nature of the mortar. As a tool, the mortar can be made of wood or mineral. Wood mortars are ideal for working with plant spirits, and mineral ones are good for working with the nature of Shadow as the organic memory of the earth.

In Witchcraft, tools should be dedicated to a specific usage or nature. This helps maintain a focus and serves as a portal for specific streams of consciousness. Part of dedicating a tool to a particular use of service requires cleansing it of any energy contamination (previous energy attachments). To consecrate any of your tools, perform the following:

Add three teaspoons of salt to a pot of boiling water and speak these words:

> "I purify this fluid essence to expel disharmony to open the entry of sacredness to all that it touches."

Remove the pot from the fire. Using a wooden spoon, dip it into the water and then sprinkle the tool. Repeat three times.

Each tool can be dedicated to a specific entity or usage as you wish. You can customize the assignment by applying the desired name to connect with the specific tool. The traditional assignments are as follows:

- Mortar and pestle: The Hallow

- Ring: She of the Thorn-Blooded Rose

- Wand: He of the Deep Wooded Places

- Knife: Three Daughters of Night

- Platter: The Hallow

- Feminine Stang: She of the White Round

- Masculine Stang: He of the Deep Wooded Places

- Broom: She of the White Round

- Cauldron: She of the Crossroads

- Ghost Stone: She of the Crossroads

As you sprinkle each tool, speak the following:

> "With this purifying water, I consecrate this tool in the name of [give name] and dedicate it to [her/his/their/its] service."

Once the tools are consecrated, treat them with the reverence due any sacred object. None of the tools may be used for non-ritual, non-magical, or non-spiritual use. When not using them, keep the tools on an altar or wrapped and put away in a drawer, cabinet, or trunk.

PREPARING AND CHARGING THE TOOLS:

Mortar and Pestle

To prepare your mortar, perform the following:

Place the mortar out beneath the full moon when it's high overhead in the night sky. Use candles for lighting during this preparation. Pour fresh water into the mortar (about two-thirds filled), and then pick it up in both hands. Hold the mortar so that the moon above you is reflected on the water. Speak these words:

> "Queen of light in the night sky bright,
> I call you to this Witch's rite.
> Enter this mortar, imbue this womb,
> Enter this mortar, imbue this tomb."

Continue holding the mortar up and turn yourself in a full circle, clockwise, saying:

> "Life Giver, womb birther, mother of all,
> Open to the lighted world, come to the call."

Next, turn in a full circle, counterclockwise, saying:

> "Death Taker, tomb maker, receiver of all,
> Open to the world of black, come to the call."

Pour the water out of the mortar directly into the earth. Next, set the mortar on the ground and replenish the water. After this, pick up the pestle in your left hand. Position yourself so that you see the moon on the surface of the water in the mortar. Then dip the pestle into the water and stir it slowly in a clockwise manner while you say:

> "Queen of light in the night sky bright,
> I call you to this Witch's rite.
> Enter this pestle, deep inside,
> Grant me the power to stir the tide."

Now, hold the pestle up to the moon and turn yourself in a full circle, clockwise, saying:

> "Horn awakener, seed bearer, generator of all,
> Rise to the lighted world, come to the call."

Next, turn in a full circle, counterclockwise, saying:

> "Serpent slumberer, life gatherer, witherer of all,
> Open to the world of black, come to the call."

Now, set the mortar and pestle down separately, side by side. Look at the moon with your left eye (right eye closed) and place your palm (left hand) beneath the moon (as though cupping it). Place the palm of your right hand over the mortar and say:

> "Mortar of the Witches' Craft, by art of magic in the night,
> To you I pass the blessed moon's bright and sacred light."

Next, place the palm of your right hand over the pestle and say:

> "Pestle of the Witches' Craft, by art of magic in the night,
> To you I pass the blessed moon's bright and sacred light."

Set the pestle inside the mortar, place both palms over the set, and say:

> Womb at the center of all things,
> Shaper, transformer, and birther of all,
> Hold or free spirits that come to the call,
> Life Giver, Death Taker,
> Stone carver, dream maker,
> I turn the Wheel, then to show,
> And what I spin, it now is so."

Clap your hands three times, place both palms back over the mortar and pestle, and say:

> "Tree at the center of all things,
> Tower from where enchantment sings,
> Thresher, dream churner, joiner of all,
> Sound for the spirits to come at my call."

Complete by drying the mortar and pestle and taking them away wrapped in a cloth.

The Witches' Ring

Among the most personal tools for a Witch is the ring of power. It serves to keep her or him in the flow of the occult current of Witchery. In Old World Witchcraft, the ring is customarily made of silver with a stone setting. The latter is selected for its symbolic meaning or ascribed energy. The most popular stones are moonstone, black onyx, tiger eye, and fire agate. Although technically not stone, amber, jet, and red coral are favored as well in a Witches' ring. The ring should be worn during each ritual, work of magic, or casting of a spell. In this way, it continues to absorb power and vitalize the Witch. Each time you connect with the ring, you draw upon all that's imbued within it.

When you have chosen your ring, anoint it with moon oil. You can make your own from a mixture of camphor and jasmine, or purchase one through a Witch shop. A simple recipe for moon oil is three parts jasmine to one part camphor. Before using it, place the oil out beneath the light of the full moon for at least an hour. This will imbue it with the virtue of the moon. The term *virtue* in occultism refers to the pure essence of something, a mystical or magical nature of a specific resonance.

The preparation of the Witches' ring is fairly simple. On the night of the full moon, at nine p.m. or midnight, empower the ring with the four creative elemental natures: earth, air, fire, and water. This requires four containers, one placed to denote each of the four sacred directions of north, east, south, and west. The north bowl will contain fresh soil or pebbles, the east bowl some smoking incense, the south bowl a lighted red votive candle, and the west bowl fresh water.

Beginning with the south bowl, pass the ring safely through the candle flame, three times, each time saying:

> "Spirit of Fire, transform this ring from a thing of earth into one of spirit."

Next, pass the ring through the incense smoke, three times, each time saying:

> "Spirit of Air, carry this ring into the mystic realm."

Now, dip the ring into the water, three times, each time saying:

> "Spirit of Water, move this ring into the current of magic."

Finish by tapping the ring on the soil or pebbles, three times, each time saying:

> "Spirit of Earth, bind all forces together to manifest the Witches' ring of power."

Pick the ring up with the left hand and extend it to the moon. Use your left eye to look through the opening of the band so that you can see the moon encircled. Then speak the words of enchantment:

> "By fire, air, water, and earth,
> Now the Witches' ring is birthed.
> Here below in this moonlit hour
> Awakens now the timeless power."

Next, link the ring to She of the Thorn-Blooded Rose. To do this, set the ring on your work area. Take a single long-stemmed red rose and use it to trace the letter *S* three times over the ring, saying:

> "In the name of She of the Thorn-Blooded Rose, may this ring be a protection and summon the forces of the Green-wood magic. I join this ring to the thicket of thorns that encircle, to the canopy of branches that shelter, and to the entangled roots that bind."

Put the ring on, stand with your arms and legs stretched out in the form of an *X*, and make the declaration:

> "I am Pharmakeute!
> Roots beneath, hear me,
> Shadow below, know me.
> Branches above, connect me,
> for in-between I stand
> as a Thorn-Blooded Witch of the Ways."

Conclude by pouring an offering of wine on the ground and pushing a coin down into the soil. You can increase the powers of the ring by using one or both of two simple methods:

1. Hold the ring in the palm of your left hand. Take a lighted stick of incense in your right hand. Using the smoke, trace a

five-pointed star (clockwise) over the ring, three times, each time saying:

"Strict charge and watch I give, that to the wearer of this
ring, no evil thing approach or enter in."

2. Place a large metal lid from a jar on your work area. Fill it half full with some perfume or cologne (180 proof grain alcohol is best if you can obtain some). Carefully touch a lighted match to the surface of the liquid. A soft blue flame should dance across its surface. Attach the ring to a metal chain and suspend it over the flame. Gently swing the ring in a circle so that it passes in and out of the fire. While doing this, speak the words of enchantment, three times:

"Fire pass into this ring as a shield,
flames of protection that do not yield."

Remove the ring from the fire, and then using the index finger of your right hand, trace a five-pointed star over it. In your mind's eye, see this as a star of blue flame—sense it. Mentally pass the blue flaming star into the ring.

This completes the magical charge. Whenever you feel threatened, hold the ring in front of you and say:

"Fire rise from this ring as a shield,
flames of protection that do not yield."

Mentally see it rise from the ring and sense its flaming presence in front of you. Remember to reload the ring with fire each full moon using the method of passing fire back into the ring.

The Witches' Blade

Among the oldest of the Witches' tools mentioned in ancient writings is the knife. Classical writings depict the Witch known as Medea using a bronze knife to harvest herbs. Other ancient depictions show the knife used on a sacrificial animal. In modern times, the customary knife is made of steel and has a black handle. Within the structure of Old World Witchcraft, the blade is never used to draw blood and is never used to physically cut anything.

Begin preparation three nights before the moon is full. Start by digging a small hole in the earth that's as deep as your hand is long. Then take equal portions of mandrake root bits, myrtle leaves, and rose thorns. The mandrake is the key that opens the doorway between the worlds, linking humankind with the Otherworld. Myrtle is the herb of the Faery Race and enlists aid in working with spirits. Rose thorns are protective agents in the Greenwood Realm. Add all three to the soil from the hole you dug and mix this all together. Then replace the soil into the hole. Leave this until the night of the full moon.

Next, boil two cups of water and then add about a teaspoon of mandrake root (bits) and myrtle leaves, along with nine red rose petals. Simmer for twenty minutes, strain, and then refrigerate the water until needed.

On the night of the full moon, begin preparing the knife for charging. Set a bowl containing the liquid herbal mixture on your work area. In order to charge the knife for use, it must first be heated over an open flame for a couple of minutes. This awakens the memory of the creative force of fire within the blade. Once the blade is hot, say these words:

"Blade of steel, your charge shall be,
to banish all I bid of Thee!"

Then immediately plunge the blade into the herbal potion. You should hear a hissing sound as hot metal meets cold water. This seals the magical intent into the knife and records the memory. Afterward, dry off the blade and set it aside.

To complete the process, you will need to magnetize the blade. Take a medium size magnet (or lodestone) and stroke it against the blade from the hilt out to the tip, firmly and moderately, nine times on each side of the blade. Do not stroke back and forth, but always in one direction. Repeat the process again, nine times, on the first side of the blade and then the opposite. As you stroke the magnet along the blade, periodically say these words:

> "Blade of steel, your charge shall be,
> to attract all things I bid of Thee!"

The final process for charging the knife is to connect it with the forces of above, below, and in-between. Begin by returning to the spot where you dug the hole. Pour the liquid herbal mixture slowly on it. Next, trace out a triangle to enclose the spot. Then grasp the handle of the dagger in both hands, with the blade pointing down, and raise your arms up to the moon, saying:

> "I am a Witch of the Old Ways,
> Stars above, bear witness,
> Moon above, look down with favor,
> Earth below, be mated with light."

Now, push the blade down into the soil (directly in the center of the hole) up to the hilt of the handle. Next, draw power down from the moon as follows:

Kneel before the moon, hands upon the thighs, and say:

> "At will I call the streams to power,
> From their fountains when sacred 'tis the hour;
> Seas swell and rest when clouds do I re-form.
> With spells and charms, the serpents do I raise,
> And from oak and boulder make known the ways.
> Whole woodlands sway and lofty mountains quake,
> Caverns open and spirits from tombs awake."

Raise your left hand and cup the moon in your palm, saying:

> "And Thee, O Moon, I draw."

Then quickly close your hand in a grasping manner, seemingly closing the moon within your hand. Do not look up at this point, but bring your closed hand down (as if drawing or pulling) and then open it to grasp the knife handle. Next, place your right hand firmly over your left and concentrate upon the knife, and sense it glowing with power. Then say:

"I join you with the forces below."

After a few moments, remove the knife from the soil, hold it up to the stars, and say:

"I join you with the forces above."

Finish by bringing the knife back down and pressing it against your solar plexus, saying:

"I join you with the forces in-between."

You can now clean the knife, wrap it in a cloth, and take it with you.

The Wand

In ancient writings, the wand is frequently mentioned as a tool used in the art of Witchcraft. In Old World Witchcraft, it's one of the tools of the Greenwood magic, and for obvious reasons it is connected to the plant realm. A wand should be selected for the type of wood and the association of that wood to occult themes as well as for the feel of the wand. It's customary that the length of the wand measures from the inside of your elbow to the end of your middle finger. You can make your own or purchase one through a Witch Shop.

If you want to make your own wand, it's best to hollow out the end and fill it with magical herbs. The hole in the wand can be sealed with wax or clay. If you purchase a wand, or one is given you as a gift, you can bathe it in an herbal potion in order to establish the herbal connection. The customary recipe calls for a brew comprised of equal parts: vervain, hyssop, and rose petals. Boil three cups of water, to which you add the herbs and a pinch of salt. Allow the herbs to steep for five minutes and then allow cooling for about ten minutes. Immediately afterward, bathe the wand in the brew (dipping it three times) and then rinse it off with fresh water. Dry the wand and set it aside.

To charge the wand, go out on the night of the full moon just after sunset and prepare an altar. Upon the altar, set two white candles near the back section (separated a few inches apart). Between the candles, place an offering of white flowers. In the center of the altar, set a bowl of fresh water, about half filled. To the right of the bowl, place some incense and a silver bell. Leave everything in place until the moon is directly overhead, roughly about midnight.

When you return, light the incense and the candles. Then lift up the flowers and state that you offer them to She of the White Round. Next, take the bowl of water and sit comfortably with it in your lap. Lift the bowl up to chest height, and look down into it, adjusting the bowl so the moon is reflected on the surface of the water. Once you see the moon clearly, close your eyes and say:

> "Light of the moon
>   That shines for me,
>   Touch within, divinity.
>   Out of the night
>   Your beam, your tower,
>   Pass now to me
>   The ancient power."

Drink some of the water, and as you do so, sense that you are taking in the magical essence of the moon's light.

Set the bowl back on the altar and pick up the wand in your left hand. Then, with your right hand, cup some of the water and pour it out over the wand, so that the water runs back into the bowl. Repeat this three times, saying each time:

> "Water that shines
>   With the moon's soft light,

Here in the dark pool
Of magic's night,
Carry to wood
The bright essence we share,
And empower this
Ritual tool of the air."

Next, extend the wand upward toward the moon and hold it there. Then take three deep breaths, exhaling out upon the wand with each breath. Sense that you are transferring the essence of the moonlight that you drank moments before. Before you draw each breath, say these words:

"Air that carries
The moon through the night,
A whispering silence
To empower this rite.
I draw down the moon
From the night and beyond,
Sealed with life's breath
In this magical wand."

The wand is now charged and ready to be finished to your personal taste. You can paint or carve symbols along the shaft, add crystals, feathers, or anything you desire. Let your intuition guide you.

The Cauldron

Many old myths speak of magical cauldrons. The Witch has long been associated with these vessels. The cauldron represents the sacred womb of the earth. It also symbolizes the mystical process of transformation. The size of the cauldron isn't important in terms of symbolism. It's only important for the Witch to establish the mystical or magical alignment.

For the Witch, the cauldron is used to manifest personal desire within the material or nonmaterial realm. It's also used to change one thing into another, not in the physical sense but in its nature. One example is to place a photo in the cauldron and turn it into the *living* connection to what shows in the photo. In other words, a photo of Stonehenge becomes the astral replica in your temple or on your shrine. Another use is to dissolve things into the cauldron, and this can be anything that needs to end, renew, or recycle.

Begin creating your connection to the cauldron by cleaning it with fresh water. This will dissolve away any impurities and will render the cauldron anew. In this way, the cauldron becomes yours in every sense of the meaning. Once the cauldron has been cleansed and dried, set it beneath the full moon (nine p.m. or midnight is customary).

Stand by the cauldron and face east. Raise your left hand up to the moon, and place the palm of your right hand over the cauldron. Walk slowly, clockwise, three times around the cauldron while saying:

"As was known and called upon in the days of old,
I draw the enchantment as in generations told."

Trace the rim of the cauldron, clockwise, with the fingers of your right hand. While doing this, say:

"Sacred cauldron, your task shall be,
Manifest all things as willed by me."

Next, trace the cauldron's rim, counterclockwise, with the fingers of the left hand, and say:

"Sacred cauldron, your task shall be,
Dissolve all things as willed by me."

Finish by placing both palms over the cauldron and saying:

"I call to She of the White Round, the Three Daughters of Night, and She of the Crossroads to imbue this cauldron with the Old Magic, and to be its tenders."

This completes the work. It's customary to leave a willow twig in the cauldron when not in use. To use the cauldron, decide what you wish to draw or release. Place its representation in the cauldron, and then trace your fingers along the rim of the cauldron (clockwise for drawing, counterclockwise for releasing). While doing this, speak your intent and what you wish to accomplish.

The Witches' Broom

The Witches' broom evolved from two old concepts associated with the plant realm. The first is rooted in the ancient practice of making an oath while placing a hand on a sacred tree. This was often performed at or near a crossroads. In the traditions of Southern Europe, a wooden pole known as a *hekataia* or *hekataeon* (named after the goddess Hecate) was erected at the crossroads. Hecate is among the oldest of goddesses associated with Witchcraft, and oaths made to her were considered inviolate. In Old World Witchery, the broom is made from ash, birch, and willow trees. The ash is the handle, the birch is the sweep, and the lashes that bind them together are willow strips.

The second concept linked to the broom is that spirits abide within plants. To enter into a relationship with a plant spirit connects you with its consciousness. Invoking or evoking a plant spirit makes it active within you and around you. When this happens, the spirit can direct and convey you in the magical or astral sense. This is called riding the spirit, which is a theme that shows up in old Witch lore. This is reflected in stories about Witches riding on sticks, plants, and even goats, on their way to the Witches' Sabbat.

In Old World Witchcraft, we ride the broom, meaning we are conveyed through states of consciousness connected with the spirits that have an affinity with the ash, birch, and willow trees. The ash, as the World Tree, opens the portals to other realms. The birch draws the ancestral allies along with the spirits of the dead. This allows for safe passage in the chthonic realms. The willow tree announces that the Witch operates under the authority of the Goddess of Witchcraft.

To prepare your broom, select or make one that's suitable to you and the art of Witchcraft. Ideally it should be made of ash, birch, and willow, but you can work with other woods. In doing so, make sure you research the traditional occult properties of the trees or plants, as this will tell you about the spirits that inhabit them. This way you will know what you are riding and what influences you have mounted.

The size of the broom can vary, but one symbolic measurement is from your feet to your heart. A rustic-looking broom will help you keep a sense of the plant realm from which the parts originate. This will enhance your sense of the Greenwood magic. The following enchantments will imbue your broom with the magical alignments needed to make it a tool of Old World Witchery.

On the night of the full moon, lay the broom down in front of you. Look up at the moon and speak the words of calling by first holding your left hand up (fingers stretched outward) just beneath the moon, and then saying:

"I call to She of the White Round."

Then close your right eye, and while looking at the moon with your left eye, slowly (and with focused intent) move your hand up and close your fingers into a fist that captures the moon. If done correctly, you cannot see the moon outside of your fist. At this point, you are ready to draw the moon down into your broom. To do this, keep your right eye closed and the moon in your hand, and then lower your gaze down to meet the broom. At this point, open the right eye so that both are looking at the broom. Speak the words of enchantment:

"To you, this broom of the Witches' Art,
I bring the light, I pass the spark."

Now, sense a firm grip on the moon and then feel as though you are slowly pulling it down from the night sky. Do this with a sense of weight and feel the muscles of your arm in play (they should literally be flexing or straining as you perform the act). As you begin this technique, speak the enchantment:

"At will I call the streams to power
From their fountains when sacred 'tis the hour;

Seas swell and rest, when clouds do I re-form.
With spells and charms, the serpents do I raise,
And from oak and boulder make known the ways.
Whole woodlands sway and lofty mountains quake,
Caverns open and spirits from tombs awake,
And Thee, O Moon, I draw."

When your hand reaches the broom, open your fist and push the moonlight into the bindings on the sweep. Hold your hand in place and speak the words of enchantment:

"Be you the broom of the Witches' Art,
Magic's arrow and moonbeam's dart.
To and fro the spirits you sweep,
Carry me to the inner realms I seek."

End by raising the broom (sweep end up) until the moon appears to sit on the edge of the bristles. Say the final words of enchantment:

"She of the White Round, above, blessing beams,
I below, and the broom in-between.
I ride above the water, and beneath the air,
In your name to places that only Witches dare."

The broom is now fully prepared. Give thanks and depart with the broom. Techniques for using it in ritual and magic are included in other chapters.

The Blackthorn Cane

A powerful tool in the Witches' arsenal is the blackthorn cane. In some traditions, it's called a thunder rod, blasting rod, or storm raiser. The Witch customarily carries the blackthorn in public as a reminder that it's best not to harass him/her. As with all untamed creatures in Nature, there's safety in leaving the Witch unprovoked. The vitality of blackthorn is its raw power that, in the hands of the Witch, is untainted or restrained by the control of social rules or by imposed ethics. In the Thorn Path of Witchery, the law is that we don't harm the innocent, but the definition of an innocent is one who doesn't provoke the Witch. Provoke, and you lose the status of being innocent.

You can make a cane from a blackthorn branch or purchase one already shaped for that purpose. Both ways should be accomplished during the three moonless nights of any month (but a favored time is when the moon is in the sign of Scorpio). When you have the blackthorn, begin its preparation on the first night of the dark moon. Lay the blackthorn down on the ground beneath the stars (they need to be visible). Hold both palms over the cane, and while looking at the stars, give the invocation:

> "Stars, ancient watchers, bear witness to what here is made,
> Proclaim in all the worlds of mortal-kind and shade."

Now, give the second call while looking at the blackthorn:

> "I call upon you, Potia (po-tee-ah), daughter of the Night,
> Look favorably upon me and aid this magic rite."

Anoint the blackthorn with master oil on both ends and the center. Then say the final words of enchantment:

> "Be now the Master's bolt in this blackthorn cane,
> A protection unto me, and for my enemies a bane."

End by taking the blackthorn to a crossroads after sunset, where you will prick the thumb of your right hand and let three drops of blood into a cup of water. Pour this on the ground in the center of the crossroads, and say:

> "Here at the crossroads in this hour,
> I claim the right of the Witches' power.
> Forces of night and shadows bold,
> The Witches' blackthorn cane I hold."

Now, strike the spot three times with the tip of the cane. Repeat this three times (the words and the triple striking). This will conclude the magical alignments. The blackthorn is now ready to use. When you want to evoke the power of the blackthorn cane, raise it high above your head, speak the words corresponding to the situation, and then strike the earth three times:

Against an Enemy

> "I see my enemies' plots, and force them rend,
> The Witches' lightning strike I now do send."

To Veil or Hide Something

> "Over this I draw the black and misty tide,
> From sight, and sound, and touch, I hereby hide."

To Bind Someone

> "I set thorns against the ill you bring,
> And close you in the thicket's ring."

To Undo Something

> "By the unseen tide I send to you,
> All you've done I now undo."

Or:

> "By the washing tide and morning dew,
> All that's come I now undo."

The Witches' Stang

In Old World Witchery, the concept of the stang is rooted in themes associated with tree veneration. In particular, the stangs used in the Rose and Thorn Path of Witchery are connected to the idea of the sacred tree within a grove sanctuary. Such groves are often dedicated to a goddess or a god. Under certain circumstances, a branch may be taken for use in the Witches' Craft. These branches become the ritual and magical tools known as stangs.

The mystical theme associated with a sacred tree centers on the priestess or priest of the grove. Her or his training, experience, and devotion is symbolized by a specific length of branch (metaphorically speaking, a period of growth). The measure of the branch is the physical height of the individual, but with one additional element. The length of the distance between the person's elbow and the tip of the middle finger is added to the overall length of the branch. This represents her or his ability and nature to extend outward into the world (and to other people). So the symbolism of the stang is the combined height of the person (representing the experience and training) with the length of the arm from elbow to fingertip. To bear the stang is to proclaim one's connection to something greater than the self: the source that shaped the Witch. With the stang in hand, the Witch is always connected to the sacred tree of the ancestors. To wield the stang is to move forces that open gateways to other realities.

In Old World Witchcraft, we use two different but related stangs, the feminine and the masculine. The feminine stang is used to trace the ritual or magical circle on the ground. This act represents placing the full moon directly on the earth through mimic magic. The moon is literally drawn down upon the ground. The stang represents the feminine forces as conceptual, seeing the wholeness. Drawing the moon on the ground evokes She of the White Round, the moon as divinity. The feminine stang, through its link to this evocation, also represents the Moon Goddess when placed upright within the ritual circle.

The masculine stang is used to open a ritually cast circle when it's created as a barrier (as opposed to simply being sacred space). Opening the circle at any given place on the perimeter allows people to enter and leave the enclosure without penetrating the membrane of the ritual space. A circle that's cast to enclose and protect can be constructed to generate an astral force field, enclosing it in an etheric sphere. An old occult teaching warns that walking through such a field without creating an opening can cause damage to the astral body of the person passing through the membrane of the circle. Use of the stang is described in chapter 8, "The Old Rites."

The masculine stang is thought of as a tool of linear consciousness. It's a tool of detail as opposed to conceptual. It's the Part, and the feminine stang is the Whole. The feminine stang creates the entire concept of the ritual circle, while the masculine stang deals with the parts of that concept.

To prepare your stangs, select branches with the measurements that suit you. You will need to make two alignments. The first is to the earth forces, and the second is to the celestial forces. This is because a stang awakens both, and it serves as a key to unlock (or lock) the portals between material and nonmaterial reality.

For the feminine stang, here are the alignments. Mark out a ritual circle, and then place the stang at the east quarter. Hold both palms toward the stang and say:

> "Hook you the moon, and carry it evermore,
> Over the land of the living, to the far distant shore."

Now, pick up the stang, turn yourself around, and carry it to the west quarter. Set it in place and say:

> "Moon on the water, all souls pass,
> Doorways open, guardians stand fast."

For the masculine stang, here are the alignments. Mark out a ritual circle, and then place the stang at the south quarter. Hold both palms toward the stang and say:

> "Hook you the Sun, and carry it evermore,
> Over the Green lands, and the sea-catching shore."

Now, pick up the stang, turn yourself around, and carry it to the north quarter. Set it in place and say:

> "Sun on the Greenwood, into life souls pass,
> Doorways open, guardians stand fast."

Lay the stangs together, place both palms over them, and say:

> "In the name of She of the Crossroads,
> be you the keys and the bars to all gateways."

This completes the alignment. The feminine stang is used to trace the ritual circle on the ground. The masculine stang is used to open an entrance from the circle when needed and to close it again. The feminine stang is stood at the north during ritual, and the masculine stang stands at the south. When placed this way, they represent the presence of the feminine and masculine divine emanations.

The Sacred Witch Stone

In Old World Witchcraft, stone is the eternal connection, the incorruptible. It's also the boundary marker. In the Rose and Thorn Path, there are two stones: the sacred stone and the ghost stone. The first is used to establish and maintain the covenant between Witches of the Ways and the entities of Old World Witchcraft. In this sense, it's symbolic of oath, dedication, and loyalty. The second use is in connection with spirits of the dead (detailed in my previous book *Old World Witchcraft*).

Ideally, the stones should be no more than three inches long. Select one to be the ghost stone and the other to be the sacred stone. Preparation begins with setting the mortar on your work area along with a bowl of fresh water. Pour the water into the mortar, filling it about half full, and then say:

> "Here is the formless, and the receiver and dissolver of all."

Next, place the stones in the mortar and say:

> "Here is the formed and everlasting, the preserver and foundation of all."

Place both palms over the mortar and say:

> "Where the formed and formless join together, there's the place of the in-between, there's the essence of magic."

Next, retrieve the ghost stone from the water, hold it in your left hand, and say:

> "I pull you from the formless into the realm of mortal-kind. Be a stone of demarcation, boundary, and binding over those between the worlds, over those in the world of the living who are now without flesh."

Set the ghost stone down and retrieve the sacred stone from the water, hold it in your left hand, and say:

> "I pull you from the formless into the world of formation. Hold to you the sacredness of the Otherworld and the Spirit of the Land in the realm of mortal-kind."

Lay the stones side by side, spaced a few inches apart, with the ghost stone on the left. Place your right palm over the ghost stone and say:

> "In the name of She of the Crossroads, I charge you with power over spirits of the dead who still dwell in the land of the living."

Place your right palm over the sacred stone, and say:

> "In the name of She of the White Round, He of the Deep Wooded Places, and by the presence of the Hallow, I charge you as the sacred center of the Round, here in the realm of mortal-kind."

Put the stones away in a pouch until needed. The sacred stone will be used in the full moon ritual, and the ghost stone will feature in working with spirits of the dead. Further information about their usage can be found in other chapters. You can also find detailed instruction in my book *Old World Witchcraft*.

The Platter

In Old World Witchcraft, the platter is used to cast spells. Ideally, it should be white in color. The platter is dusted with ash that covers its face. A finger is used to draw plant spirit symbols in the ash. As the ash is moved away by the finger, the color of the plate is revealed, and this makes the symbol stand out. In most spells, the ash is blown into the wind to send forth the magical request, which is enhanced with the power of the plant spirit.

The ash used in platter work is made from burning dried leaves. The type of plant used is in accord with the nature of the spell. For example, mint is excellent for communication, rue for prosperity, roses for love, and any thorn-bearing plant for protection. Activate the platter by presenting it to the east quarter as you say: "Spirit of the air, I ask you to empower this object with the ability to send its magic into the wind."

To fully appreciate the value of plants in Witchcraft, we need to understand the connection between them, the spirits that inhabit them, and the covenant that joins the Witch with the Green Realm. To that end, let's turn to the next chapter.

4

PLANT SPIRITS OF THE GREENWOOD

In many ancient tales, people are turned into trees or plants. Old lore contains stories of plants springing up from the blood of heroes or deities. All of this speaks to an intimate connection between plants and humans that's not reliant upon any material value per se. Instead, the basis of these myths appears to address something spiritual and mystical in nature. But not all stories are about humans becoming plants; the mandrake is a plant that forms a human shape as though it seeks to become one. We will examine the mandrake later in this chapter and examine it as a plant spirit. This will also demonstrate its importance in Witchcraft.

Plant spirits appear in the most ancient practices of Witchcraft. These primal entities possess power and knowledge that aids the Witches' Craft. Plants have long been associated with Witchcraft, and the most well-known include aconite, henbane, hemlock, belladonna, foxglove, and hellebore. What isn't commonly revealed in old sources is the connection between such plants and the spirits residing within them. This mystical and magical component of working with plants is one of the previously secret arts of Witchcraft.

From a mystical perspective, we can say that spirits who once inhabited the primal forests invited humans into awareness and communication. This idea sheds a particular light on how humans learned many things about plants before the time of science. Through the course of the relationship between plant spirits and Witches, a formal practice arose involving the traditional plants of Witchcraft. This practice included a working knowledge of the effects of various plants, but it also involved communicating with plant spirits.

Plant spirits comprise a component of the enduring primordial consciousness of the plant realm. They thrive even in modern cities where cement and asphalt dominate the land. Through contact with plant spirits, we can cleanse and refresh the mind, body, and soul. We can merge with the Ancestral Spirit of those who lived within the Greenwood knowledge and wisdom. In this we can reclaim the spiritual lineage of the Shaman, Witch, and Mystic, and we can remove the obstacles that prevent or weaken the flow of the river of blood that empowers each living generation.

It's not only the red blood of humankind that's of concern; there's also the importance of the green blood of plant-kind. Both of these are currents that flow from one generation to the next. In the mystical sense, fluids are the essence. They are formless but can be given formation within a shape or structure. This is similar to the idea that a soul enters into a flesh body and animates its form but is never truly the body.

THE PLANT SPIRITS

There are seventeen primary plant spirits to call upon in the Art of Witchcraft. For many centuries, they have been intimately linked to Witchcraft in myth, lore, and legend. Several of them have a foreboding public reputation associated with the potentially deadly nature of the plants they inhabit. The Witch sees past this fear and understands the ways in which a mutually beneficial rapport can be established.

The spiritual tradition of Witches working with plants centers on establishing a rapport with a powerful spirit known as She of the Thorn-Blooded Rose (previously mentioned in another chapter). This spirit connects the Witch to spirits in the plant realm and serves to safeguard the Witch against any mishaps. The roots of this relationship are entangled with the rose as a mystical symbol. While the rose has its own plant spirit named Rhondonna, She of the Thorn-Blooded Rose is the spirit of the Rose Mysteries. These mysteries use the rose as a symbol of something quite beyond the plant.

The Mystery Rose is a composite of white and red roses. The outer petals are red, representing (in part) the Material Realm. The inner petals on the blossom are white, symbolizing the spiritual realm, and more specifically the Faery World. In the center of the blossom is a black pentagon shape denoting the Hidden Realm that's known in the Rose and Thorn Path as Shadow, the organic memory of the earth. The red and white colors are the blood lineage and the spiritual lineage, a mystical heritage of those who follow the Path. With the colors of black, red, and white joined together, the Rose and Thorn Path takes its place among the oldest societies to use this occult triformity.

The rose has long been a symbol of secrecy, and the term *sub rosa* (meaning "under the rose") is used to indicate that nothing said in its presence is to be repeated. This secrecy extends to the idea of sacredness, the need to keep something separate from the commonplace world. In this regard, the rose symbolizes the blossoming of enlightenment, the attainment of spiritual understanding and realization. To hold the sacred rose is to stand as one who has been tested by thorns.

The mystical covenant with the plant realm is initiated when the Witch gives three drops of her or his blood to the rose bush. It awakens the spirits, and they accept the offering of the human vital essence. This stirs the ancient memory of the Pharmakeute, the Witches of the Old World who once venerated the plant spirits so long ago. The plant spirits remember, rise to meet the Witch, and to know one another again.

The renewal of oaths taken in the presence of the rose brings the Witch into the care of She of the Thorn-Blooded Rose. Going forth under her name, the Witch enters the plant realm and is immersed in the Greenwood magic. Through this, the Witch is brought before the spirits of Old World Witchcraft, the powerful spirits of the ancient plants of the Pharmakeute.

There's a very old connection between Witches and roses, but it's not a direct one per se. It has to do with the goddess Venus, who is often thought of as a goddess of love. Historian Albert Grenier, in his book *The Roman Spirit*, comments that Venus was apparently once an ancient garden goddess. Likewise, historian Cyril Bailey remarks in *Phases in the Religion of Ancient Rome* that Venus was formerly a protector of gardens and fruit trees. This is where the Witch, as an herbalist, connects with Venus. It's noteworthy that in old tales, Witches were sought after for love potions (which were made from plants).

In some forms of Traditional Witchcraft, we find Dame Venus, who appears as the consort of Lucifer the light bearer. She's also featured in medieval tales in which she takes on themes often associated with Faery lore, such as a realm within a hollow hill and travelers falling into enchantment. There's also a possible link between Dame Venus and the Sibyl of Cumae, an oracle priestess associated with the god Apollo. She leads the Trojan hero Aeneas through the Underworld on a quest, and it's noteworthy that his mother is Aphrodite/Venus. Author C. J. S. Thompson, in his book *Mystic Mandrake*, writes:

> It's supposed that mandragora acquired its reputation as a potent love-charm on account of its association with Circe, as it was sometimes called "the plant of Circes" after the sorceress. The connection of the plant with the mysteries of love is said by some to account for Aphrodite being known at times as Mandragoritis, or "She of the Mandragora." ... Hesychius refers to the "Lady of the Mandrake," which, it's claimed, substantiates the suggestion of its association with Aphrodite.

There are stepping-stones worthy of integration. They consist of the time-honored connection between the rose flower and Venus, the association of Venus with gardens, and the relationship between plants and Witches. There's a spiritual tradition linked to each of these stepping-stones. They lead to the Witches' rapport with spirits that dwell in the traditional plants of Witchcraft.

Working with plant spirits requires a preestablished connection with She of the Thorn-Blooded Rose and entering into the covenant of the blood. This is a simple method but one that's very sacred in Old World Witchcraft.

Within the Greenwood Realm, and through the Greenwood Magic, you can encounter the powerful spirit known as She of the Thorn-Blooded Rose. Within occult philosophy we find the principle of initiatory forces, which work to connect people with Otherworld influences. Such forces can be tapped through formal rites of initiation, and they can also be embraced through direct communication with spirits or deities.

The rose has long been a symbol of secrecy, devotion, and enlightenment. The spirit known as She of the Thorn-Blooded Rose is linked to this nature through her connection to the Witch as a Pharmakeute. This nature is the Witch in spiritual relationship with the plant world as opposed to simply being an herbalist. In other words, the Witch works with both the material and nonmaterial aspects of plants.

The relationship with She of the Thorn-Blooded Rose begins with the blood covenant. This binds humankind with plant-kind, and establishes She of the Thorn-Blooded Rose as an ally. Through her, you can meet and create relationships with other plant spirits. The blood covenant begins with an exchange of the red blood for the green blood. This is accomplished through pricking a finger and squeezing three drops of blood into a small container of water. The mixture is poured out onto the base of a rose bush. The covenant is completed by drinking a sip of liquid chlorophyll (the green blood) in front of the rose bush. The words of joining are:

> "Blood to blood, make kindred One,
> Beneath the moon, beneath the sun.
> Plant and flesh, spirit and soul,
> Bound to ways that make us whole."

To begin working directly with She of the Thorn-Blooded Rose, you should use the pentagon figure as a doorway. This configuration naturally appears in the center of a five-pointed star.

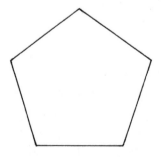

Draw the figure and color it red, for this is the level of the rose connection. Mystically speaking, beneath it lays the white door of the bone memory and the black door of the organic memory of the earth residing at the very core of Shadow. On the center of the pentagon, mark the symbol of She of the Thorn-Blooded Rose, and next to it place a fresh red rose.

Take three rose leaves and join them with thread and needle, passing the threaded needle through the center of the leaves. Now, form a triangle around the leaves using rose petals (with the threaded-leaves in its center). Next, set the red pentagon in front of the rose petal triangle (oriented with one tip toward the triangle figure). In the center of the pentagon, place a lighted black candle—this will represent Shadow beneath the earth.

Using the index finger of your left hand, trace a triangle above and over the flame, at a safe distance, and speak the words of conjuration:

> "She of the Thorn-Blooded Rose, I call to you in Shadow deep,
> Awaken now, my red lady, from your slumbered sleep.
> Open the passage to where all is hidden in the Green
> And take me to the secret world that lies in-between."

Pick up the red rose and gently inhale its scent. This is the spirit of She of the Thorn-Blooded Rose passing into your being. Do this with that intention and with great reverence.

Next, pull off one of the petals, and then roll it between your fingers using a fingernail to open its flesh. When your finger is damp with it, use the index finger on your left hand to anoint your forehead with the liquid. This opens your spirit eyes.

At this phase, you will need to commune with She of the Thorn-Blooded Rose, and by doing so, you can create the necessary rapport needed to work successfully within the Green Realm. Don't rely on visualization, but instead simply try to sense things around and in you. This is the organic approach versus that of the mind.

Begin by closing your eyes and holding the rose in your hand. Gently touch the rose to your face and other exposed areas of skin. Feel this in the sense that She of the Thorn-Blooded Rose is touching you. Then, with eyes still closed, use your fingers to lightly touch the rose. Do this with the feeling that you are touching the flesh of She of the Thorn-Blooded Rose.

Finish by sitting with the rose cupped in your left hand, and remain receptive to communication, thoughts, and feelings. Do not try to make that happen or try to rush things. Remain peaceful and waiting to see what comes. When you are ready to finish, kiss the rose and lay it in front of you. Thank She of the Thorn-Blooded Rose for being present (no matter what your experience was). The more you work with this technique, the more it will produce.

MEETING THE SPIRITS

Once you have established a rapport with She of the Thorn-Blooded Rose, you can begin to meet other plant spirits. Always make an offering of three drops of your blood in exchange for a sip of the green blood when asking her to introduce you to another spirit. Always perform the introduction before evoking a plant spirit for magical or ritual purposes. The technique calls for the creation of a black pentagon figure, which represents Shadow.

Let's use the mandrake as an example of being introduced to a spirit. There's a female and a male spirit to meet and to work with in this first stage. Begin by holding a single long-stemmed rose in your left hand and then calling upon She of the Thorn-Blooded Rose as you did in the rapport technique:

"She of the Thorn-Blooded Rose, I call to you in Shadow deep,
Awaken now, my red lady, from your slumbered sleep.
Open the passage to where all is hidden in the Green
And take me to the secret world that lies in-between."

Using rose petals, mark out a triangle on your work area. Place the seal of the Mandrake Spirit in the center of the triangle.

Speak these words as you look upon the seal:

"She of the Thorn-Blooded Rose, you I do entreat,
Present me to this spirit who now I choose to meet."

Pick up the mandrake seal and hold it in your left hand. Close your eyes and mentally picture the spirit (you can use the Mandrake Spirit drawing in this chapter as a model; select either female or male, and later you can connect with the other). Sit receptively and, with eyes still closed, seek to sense a presence. Then after a few moments, place the seal on the black pentagon gateway.

Place the palm of your right hand on top of the mandrake seal. Next, firmly press the seal in the sense that you are pushing it down into Shadow, and then say these words:

"I place the mystic seed into shadowed places deep,
Spirit of the Mandrake, bring teachings in my sleep."

Put the seal with the pentagon underneath your pillow and leave it there for three nights (and only three to begin with). Have a notebook nearby into which you can record a dream or message when you awake (and do so immediately before it might slip away). In this phase, the spirits will initiate communication. Later on, you can encounter them in waking reality, ask questions of them, receive teachings, and build your relationship. You can use this method of working with plant spirits of any type simply by using the appropriate seal and the spirit imagery. Naturally, you will say the appropriate name for each spirit when speaking over the plant seal (as you did with the mandrake example).

When working with the introduction method, it's likely that your sleep will be restless at first. You may even find that you awaken around three a.m. and can't fall back to sleep until after four a.m. This is natural, so do not be overly concerned, but be prepared for not being fully awake and refreshed in the morning.

THE PLANT SPIRITS OF OLD WORLD WITCHCRAFT

If you have performed the alignment to She of the Thorn-Blooded Rose and worked through the process of being introduced to the plant spirits, you can now begin calling upon them for aid. The following is a list of the traditional plant spirits of Witchcraft.

Atonen, Spirit of Hemlock

The spirit of hemlock is called Atonen (pronounced: a-tone-in), and it serves to make reparations for wrongdoings. It's, in essence, a spirit of redemption. This spirit most often appears as a human male figure with plant features. He's evoked on a Saturday at the beginning of any even hour of the day or night.

The Call of Enchantment

"You are he who sets all right,
Judged in day, and so in night.
Outraged cries are put to rest,
The scales are tipped with but a breath.
Misdeeds cower for fear of your hand,

A deadly price will always stand.
A debt created is a debt so made,
The leafy hand turns warm flesh to shade.
Come to the Thorn-Blooded Witch who hails,
I call you to pass through the verdant veils.
I reach out from the time-honored power,
By seed, sprout, budded leaf, and flower."

Atropa, Spirit of Nightshade

The spirit of nightshade is called Atropa (pronounced: a-trow-pah) and serves to either keep or reveal secrets of any kind. In this way, it's a cloaking spirit of the night who can reveal through drawing lunar light. The spirit usually appears as a human female figure with plant features. She's evoked on a Monday at the hours of three, six, or nine.

"You are she of the Hidden Night,
   Where shadows form in the mystic light.
   Beauty in the leafy glade and glen,
   Where life is gathered in, to return yet once again.
   Giver of visions, dream-gifter Queen,
   Peering into all that never can be seen.
   Blackness gathers as a great hooded cloak,
   Hushing the ancient words that must always remain unspoke.
   Come to the Thorn-Blooded Witch who hails,
   I call you to pass through the verdant veils.
   I reach out from the time-honored power,
   By seed, sprout, budded leaf, and flower."

Brydethe, Spirit of Birch

The spirit of birch is called Brydethe (pronounced: bree-death) and serves to direct the dead. Contacting the dead is among the oldest arts of Witchcraft. Brydethe appears as a human female figure with tree features. She's evoked in the night any time after sunset, but the most favorable times are Saturday, any full moon, and on November Eve.

The Call of Enchantment

> "You are she who calls the Crossing Ones when Death plays
> its final tune,
> The White Tree shows the rebirth path across branches to
> the moon.
> Souls fall away from life like leaves on Autumn days,
> All return again to life to walk in learnful ways.
> Silently, bark peels away, a withering release of form,
> What falls away in a season, is in another born.
> Roots pull away, nothing is bound, and all is free,
> Souls are gathered in the night, a guided moonlit journey.
> Come to the Thorn-Blooded Witch who hails,
> I call you to pass through the verdant veils.
> I reach out from the time-honored power,
> By seed, sprout, budded leaf, and flower."

Ellebrina, Spirit of Hellebore

The spirit of hellebore is called Ellebrina (pronounced: el-lah-bree-nah) and serves to calm disturbances of any kind but particularly involving spirits. This spirit takes on the form of a human female with plant features. She's evoked on a Sunday any time of day or night.

HELLEBORE

ᏸᎥᎥᏏᏃᏉᎯᏇ

The Call of Enchantment

"You are she who calms the tempest storm,
Like Yule Tide hearths with fires warm.
Breath that lulls the spirit's sleep,
In woods, halls, and huts, the peace to keep.
The Faery shimmer, the humming loom,
Enchanted songs that drift beneath a halo moon.
To ride the twig through chimney top,
And find the world where time has stopped.
Come to the Thorn-Blooded Witch who hails,
I call you to pass through the verdant veils.
I reach out from the time-honored power,
By seed, sprout, budded leaf, and flower."

Gebanshen, Spirit of Wolfbane

The spirit of wolfbane is called Gebanshen (pronounced: gebh-ann-shin) and serves to banish anything unwanted (particularly enemies and predators). This spirit most often appears as a human male figure with plant features. He's evoked on a Tuesday at any time of day or night.

The Call of Enchantment

"You are he who chases off the foe,
   Pacing the boundaries to and fro.
   Hunter becomes hunted, in silence or in sound,
   Those who hide in forest are forced to open ground.
   Cowled One, brewer of endless sleep,
   Rider of rushing arrows—distant far and deep.

The Kindred of the Hood, hidden eyes that see,
Those who set the trap, turn on foot to flee.
Come to the Thorn-Blooded Witch who hails,
I call you to pass through the verdant veils.
I reach out from the time-honored power,
By seed, sprout, budded leaf, and flower."

Kwethanna, Spirit of Hawthorn

The spirit of hawthorn is called Kwethanna (pronounced: quee-thaw-nah), and it serves to guard portals and to make them accessible to the true seekers. This spirit most often appears as a human female figure with plant features. She's evoked on a Wednesday at the beginning of any even hour of the day or night.

"You are the opener of gateways hidden and seen,
Revealing paths by moon and starlight's gleam.
Hinge holder, pivot, all is held fast,
The arm that halts or allows one to pass.
White thorn that becomes the Faery lance,
Held by the sentinel with piercing glance.
The Queen-granted bough, held to pass through,
For one whose word and heart is true.
Come to the Thorn-Blooded Witch who hails,
I call you to pass through the verdant veils.
I reach out from the time-honored power,
By seed, sprout, budded leaf, and flower."

Maestra, Spirit of Aconite

The spirit of aconite is called Maestra (pronounced: may-ess-trah), and it serves to bring forth Shadow, the organic memory of the earth. In this role, Maestra can be called upon to imbue ritual and magical tools, aligning them with the crossroads mistress. This spirit most often appears as a human female figure with plant features. She's evoked on a Monday at the beginning of any uneven hour of the night.

The Call of Enchantment

> "You are she of that most feared in the night,
> Moonless eve in forest, or brightest in moonlight.
> The dread of life or the fear of death,
> In the deep wooded places all come to rest.
> Teacher of shadowed things, old mysteries abound,
> When moon is drawn below and lies upon the ground.
> The Witching Cup is passed at the hour in-between,
> She of the White Round rises, and all know her as their Queen.
> Come to the Thorn-Blooded Witch who hails,
> I call you to pass through the verdant veils.
> I reach out from the time-honored power,
> By seed, sprout, budded leaf, and flower."

Mandragora, Spirit of Mandrake

The spirit of mandrake is known as Mandragora and has a twin known as Mandragoro. The mandrake is the only traditional plant of Witchcraft that possesses two distinct spirits and appears in the form a female or male human with plant features. The mandrake spirit serves to link humankind with plant-kind and is therefore a magical bridge to the Greenwood Realm and the space of Shadow from which all mysteries flow. In legend, the mandrake is known as the Sorcerer's Root and connects its possessor with the Old Magic. The mandrake spirit's evoked on a Monday any time of night.

MANDRAKE

ᔕᖉᑯᑲᖉᖙᗩᒼᑯᖉᖙ

MANDRAKE

ᔕᖉᑯᑲᖉᖙᗩᒼᑯᖉᑲᑯ

"You are the Master at watch in the midnight hour,
The Sorcerer's Root of the Witches' power.
The plant who wanted human form,
Brings plant and Witch to covenants sworn.
Rooted dweller in the black earth unseen,
Hidden eyes peering to catch the moon's beam.
Leafy crown of stars, the Greenwood might,
Empowers the Will through the Witches' rite.
Come to the Thorn-Blooded Witch who hails,
I call you to pass through the verdant veils.
I reach out from the time-honored power,
By seed, sprout, budded leaf, and flower."

Necterra, Spirit of Henbane

The spirit of henbane is known as Necterra (pronounced: neck-tear-rah) and serves to bind anyone who troubles you. This spirit takes on a female human form with the features of a plant. She's evoked on a Saturday any time of day or night.

The Call of Enchantment

"You are she who binds what shall not pass,
Holding all who provoke, firm and fast.
Harmful acts, hurtful words, wagging tongues are tied,
Sewn tight the ill intent, binding all who speak in lies.
Roped to posts are all who prey,
No release by night and not by day.
Hunter is hunted and captured here,
Dispatched away, nothing now to fear.
Come to the Thorn-Blooded Witch who hails,
I call you to pass through the verdant veils.
I reach out from the time-honored power,
By seed, sprout, budded leaf, and flower."

Reudwyn, Spirit of Rowan

The spirit of rowan is called Reudwyn (pronounced: rude-win) and serves to protect against enchantments. It appears in the form of a human female with plant features. Reudwyn is evoked on a Tuesday at the beginning of any even hour of the day or night.

The Call of Enchantment

"You are she who grasps enchantment in the mystic haze,
Protecting all who honor those of the ancient ways.
Star-charmed, red warning, all ill plans you rend,
Foes receive back in full measure whatever they do send.
Spell-catching boughs spread out in the day and night,
Pulling down each baneful magic work or rite.

Witch blood flows to all in line, the living bright red charm,
A promise made, a promise paid, and all are kept from harm.
Come to the Thorn-Blooded Witch who hails,
I call you to pass through the verdant veils.
I reach out from the time-honored power,
By seed, sprout, budded-leaf, and flower."

Rhondonna, Spirit of Rose

The spirit of the rose is called Rhondonna (pronounced: rown-don-nah), and it serves to preserve secrecy, agreements, and oaths. It appears in the form of a human female with plant features. Rhondonna is evoked on a Friday at the beginning of any hour of the day or night.

ROSE

budddaaq

The Call of Enchantment

"You are she of the heartfelt ways,
   petals of devotion strewn since ancient were the days.
   Oaths that are spoken, beneath your blood-red bloom,
   Bind through life and death, and to the rebirth womb.
   Joiner and binder, hearts and souls do blend,
   To meet, know, and remember, and then to love again.
   The double rose mysteries, the white rose and the red,
   All the mythic thorns are touched, and all the Witches bled.
   Come to the Thorn-Blooded Witch who hails,
   I call you to pass through the verdant veils.
   I reach out from the time-honored power,
   By seed, sprout, budded leaf, and flower."

Sheadwa, Spirit of Blackthorn

The spirit of the blackthorn is called Sheadwa (pronounced: sheed-wah), and it serves to bring forth raw power that's not attached to restrictions of any kind. It appears in the form of a human male with plant features. Sheadwa is evoked on a Monday or a Tuesday at the beginning of any odd hour.

The Call of Enchantment

"You are he of the shadows, wielder of the moon's cold wane,
From your leafy hand you pass the thunderous thorny cane.
Enemies scatter, the warrior's spiked fight,
Foes find they stand alone in blackness void of light.
Black needles poised like allies to the call,
Any you are sent against will most surely fall.

Thickets form and block all ways with woeful hedge,
In the night the black stalker comes now to avenge.
Come to the Thorn-Blooded Witch who hails,
I call you to pass through the verdant veils.
I reach out from the time-honored power,
By seed, sprout, budded leaf, and flower."

Tylanna, Spirit of Foxglove

The spirit of foxglove is named Tylanna (pronounced: tie-lah-nah), and it serves to open or restore communication between the mortal world and the Faery Realm. It also brings things, people, and beings into relationship with one another. Tylanna appears in the form of a human female with plant features. She's evoked on a Monday or a Wednesday at the beginning of any even hour.

"You are she who brings forth the sound of the moon,
That only the Fey can hear.
The gateway opens to your ancient tune,
And the Faery appear to the Seer.
Purple bells ring in the black sacred night,
And moving in Shadow, the Lantra bear light.
The dewy moon beads all do glisten,
Unveiling mystical ways to all who will listen.
Come to the Thorn-Blooded Witch who hails,
I call you to pass through the verdant veils.
I reach out from the time-honored power,
By seed, sprout, budded leaf, and flower."

Wealhenin, Spirit of Walnut

The spirit of walnut is named Wealhenin (pronounced: wheel-hay-nin), and it serves to bring people into contact with what they need at the time. It appears in the form of a human male and is evoked on a Wednesday or a Thursday at any time of the day or night.

The Call of Enchantment

> "You are he who gives the needed thing,
> Evokes Old Magic like a Witch's ring.
> Sabbat dancer, quest master, spirit's cradle,
> The shell that's the Witches' ladle.
> Shadowy branches that point the way,
> Black sacred night covers the bright blessed day.
> Gifter of the Solstice brew, the green drink of delight,
> The spirit enters deep within, to light the moonless night.
> Come to the Thorn-Blooded Witch who hails,
> I call you to pass through the verdant veils.
> I reach out from the time-honored power,
> By seed, sprout, budded leaf, and flower."

Welignwyn, Spirit of Willow

The spirit of willow is called Welignwyn (pronounced: wah-lee-gwen), and it serves to connect one with a higher nature and to establish true honor and fealty. Welignwyn also serves to enforce the sworn oath. The willow spirit appears in the form of a human female and is evoked on a Monday or a Thursday at the beginning of any even hour of the day or night.

The Call of Enchantment

> "You are she who hears the words we quoth,
> Whispered in the Night, the sacred moon oath.
> The starry night designs the Path we must find,
> A weeping tree brings forth the strips that will bind.
> Three heads adorned with the moon's white locks,

The breath from lips that utter, but never talks.
Enchanted, entwined to all that liberates,
Standing at the crossroads, the Witch there awaits.
Come to the Thorn-Blooded Witch who hails,
I call you to pass through the verdant veils.
I reach out from the time-honored power,
By seed, sprout, budded leaf, and flower."

Benya, Spirit of Vervain

The spirit of vervain is called Benya (pronounced: ben-yaw), and it serves to bring humans into contact with the Faery Race. The spirit of vervain appears in the form of a human female with plant features. She is evoked on a Monday or Friday any hour after sunset.

VERVAIN

ᴜᴅbᴀᴅզ

The Call of Enchantment

> "You are she of the covenant between Witches and the Fey,
> made in times of old, and held true to this day.
> Stewards in the mortal realm, and the Faery Land beyond,
> history turns to legend, and legend into a song.
> The Greenwood emblem of the Faeries' Creed,
> blossom of the World that lies unseen and in-between.
> Hollow hills, and hollow trees, all the hidden ways,
> mortals and Far-Country ones they knew in ancient days.
> Come to the Thorn-Blooded Witch who hails,
> I call you to pass through the verdant veils.
> I reach out from the time-honored power,
> By seed, sprout, budded leaf, and flower."

Trinua, Spirit of Rue

The spirit of rue is called Trinua (pronounced: trin-new-ah) and serves to deflect and dissipate ill-intended enchantments. The spirit of rue appears in the form of a human female with plant features. She is evoked on a Monday, Tuesday, or Saturday at any time of day or night.

Call of Enchantment

"You are she who dispels all envy and ill intent,
  defender at the watch, until all venom is spent.
  Garden sentinel, purifier of the brew,
  carried as the sign of one of the secret few.
  The Greenwood emblem of the Witches' Creed
  tree of the World that lies unseen and in-between.
  Triple branches, ill enchantments bane,

gifts of the White Round Lady are there for the Witches'
claim.
Come to the Thorn-Blooded Witch who hails,
I call you to pass through the verdant veils.
I reach out from the time-honored power,
By seed, sprout, budded-leaf, and flower."

EVOKING PLANT SPIRITS

Items needed:

Plant seal

Plant or image of plant (or plant spirit drawing)

Handful of garden soil

Liquid chlorophyll

Cup of water (half full)

Thorn or lancet (to prick skin)

Mortar & Pestle set

Whenever you want to connect with a plant spirit, select its specific seal (see Appendix A). Draw it on a piece of parchment or parchment tone paper on the day or night that's ascribed to the spirit. Take
note of any particular hour that appears in the correspondences. If
you have the physical plant, then use it as a focal point (taking full
and complete measures to protect yourself against toxins or allergies).
Whenever the plant isn't available, or should be avoided, you can use
an image of the actual plant and the plant spirit drawing (see chapter
5, "Works of Magic," for the explanation of the connection shared
by all things). I strongly urge that you use only the plant seals of any
poisonous or toxic plants and not the plants themselves unless you
are highly skilled with working with these plants. The chemicals in
the traditional plants of Witchcraft are not forgiving or apologetic.
Therefore, be safe and sane, and work with their spirits.

When you are ready to work with plant spirits, assemble all the objects on the list of needed items. Place them within easy reach. Then lay the plant seal on your working area and, using some fresh soil, make a triangle around the seal. On the opposite side of this, set the plant image or spirit drawing. In other words, the seal and triangle are between you and the plant or the image.

Place the mortar in front of you, and then lower the pestle inside. With it, make a slow back-and-forth rhythmic tapping against the mortar to accompany the words of alignment spoken in tempo:

"Seed to earth,
Earth to root,
Root to sprout,
Sprout to leaf,
Leaf to bud,
Bud to flower,
Flower to fruit,
Fruit to seed,
Seed to earth."

Now, raise the mortar over the plant seal and say:

"Womb at the center of all things,
Shaper, transformer, and birther of all,
Hold or free spirits that come to the call.
Life Giver, Death Taker,
Stone carver, Dream maker,
I turn the wheel, then to show,
And what I spin, it now is so."

Hold the pestle upright in the mortar and say:

"Tree at the center of all things,
Tower from where enchantment sings,
Thresher, dream churner, joiner of all,
Sound for the spirits to come at my call."

Place the mortar and pestle down. Next, prick a finger with the thorn or lancet and squeeze out three drops of blood in the cup of water. Then add three drops of liquid chlorophyll. Set this in front of the plant or its seal. Next, using the pestle, rap three times against the inside edge of the mortar. Then use the pestle to trace over the triangle (clockwise from top and back again). After this, point the pestle at the plant seal, and give the Call of Enchantment for the plant spirit you have chosen to call.

Once the call is given, pick the plant seal up with your left hand. Take the pestle up in your right hand and dip its tip into the cup of water. Trace the rim of the mortar with the tip of the pestle and say:

> "Spirit of [name the plant] who I call [say name spirit], join with me in this work of magic."

Now, set the plant seal in the mortar, rest the pestle on it, and say:

> "By the authority of She of the Thorn-Blooded Rose, and through the covenant of the red and green blood, be now under my direction until I release your seal."

All that remains now is to look directly at the plant or plant/spirit image and describe what you want the spirit to perform for you. Keep this simple and use as few words as possible. Maintain the seal within the mortar for twenty-four hours, and then release your connection. To release the seal, pour fresh water into the mortar. Let it stand until the paper is thoroughly soaked. Then remove the seal and roll it between your fingers. Squeeze and shape it into a ball, and then bury it in the ground. This will fully release the plant spirit. Clean the mortar and pestle, and put them away for future use.

THE WITCHES' FAMILIAR SPIRIT

Witches have long been associated with a familiar spirit of one type or another. This type of spirit connects the Witch to the Otherworld or a source of power, or it serves as an ally in the life and work of the

Witch. In Old World Witchcraft, this is a spiritual connection and the Witch works to form an intimate bond with the spirit. In this sense, a familiar spirit is one whose nature is known to the Witch through personal contact and experience.

In some traditions of Witchcraft, the familiar spirit takes the form of an animal, and these often appear in folklore as a mouse, hare, toad, cat, or bird (to name but a few). In the Rose and Thorn Path of Witchery, the Witch is the Pharmakeute, the knower of plants. Therefore, the plant spirit takes on the role of the familiar. Although live plants are used because of the spirit that inhabits them, the Witch carries a root as the perpetual magical link. This enables the Witch to always be in contact with the chosen plant and its spirit. The root is customarily carried in a small pouch that's usually kept out of plain sight.

After meeting the plant spirits through the aid of She of the Thorn-Blooded Rose, you may find one in particular that calls to you (one you feel more drawn to than others). If not, you can select one based solely upon its magical nature. To begin, you will need a piece of mandrake root. This is the safest of the roots to work with, as most of the traditional plants of Witchcraft are too deadly to touch. The mandrake is half plant and half human (in the mystical sense) and will serve as a link to all other plants. In other words, it becomes an ally.

To connect with a familiar spirit, you will need the following items:

Mandrake plant seal

Seal of the plant spirit chosen as a familiar

Image of the spirit drawing

A thorn or lancet (for pricking a finger)

A cup of water

Handful of fresh garden soil

Liquid chlorophyll

A long stem rose

Obtain your mandrake root sometime during the three nights of the dark moon (when it cannot be seen). Do not take the entire root, as this will kill the plant. If that happens, the spirit of the plant will not hold you in favor and might likely cause you problems afterward. Uncover some of the root and ask permission of the plant to cut a piece of it off; do so quickly in order to minimize trauma. Once severed, put the soil back around the root and make an offering to the plant with some water mixed with three drops of your blood. If you are using dried mandrake from an outside source, place it in a small bowl with some liquid chlorophyll. This will help reanimate the spirit of the plant.

When you are ready, place the root on the palm of your left hand, and then hold it up to the sky. Speak the words of enchantment:

> "Starry night, bear witness from above, and imbue this root with your all-seeing light."

Lower the root and touch it to the earth. Then speak the enchantment:

> "All you who dwell in the hidden roots below, imbue this root with your far-reaching arms."

Summon the mandrake spirit by placing its seal on the ground and using soil to enclose it in a triangle figure. Use the thorn to prick your finger, mix three drops of your blood with the green plant blood (chlorophyll) in a cup, and then pour half of it out in front of the mandrake seal.

Using your right hand, hold the root over the mandrake seal and say:

> "I summon to me the spirit of the Mandrake."

Now, pick up the mandrake seal in your left hand and speak the words of calling:

> "Come to the Thorn-Blooded Witch who hails,
> I call you to pass through the verdant veils.

I reach out from the time-honored power,
By seed, sprout, budded leaf, and flower."

Next, place the mandrake seal and root in the mortar. Then place the seal of the plant intended to be your familiar in the triangle of soil. Take the pestle up in your right hand and dip its tip into the remaining water in the cup. Trace the rim of the mortar with the tip of the pestle, and say:

"Spirit of [name the plant] who I call [say name spirit], join with me in this work of magic."

Now, add the seal to the mortar, dry the pestle, and then hold it out in front of you like a wand. Use the Call of Enchantment for the chosen plant spirit (as given in the previous section of this chapter) to summon the desired familiar spirit. When finished, rest the pestle on the seal inside of the mortar, pick up the rose, and say:

"By the authority of She of the Thorn-Blooded Rose, and through the covenant of the red and green blood, be now under my direction until I release your seal."

To conclude, hold the rose in your right hand and the mortar in the left. Sit and commune with the plant familiar. Use the image of the plant spirit as a focal point until you feel it's no longer needed. While you sit with the rose and the mortar that holds the plant seal, you can talk to the familiar, give it instructions, or simply try to merge with it in a spiritual connection. Once rapport has been established, you will no longer need this formal method of evoking the familiar. It will simply come when you call it, and it may come on its own as well from time to time.

5

WORKS OF MAGIC

The arts of Thorn-Path Witchery belong to the night and to the moon. They are, however, rooted in the Greenwood magic. This is the "Old Magic" of our ancestors, the connection to the living forces that join all things together. It's drawn up from the network of roots, passed into the green blood of all plants, and released in vaporous form from the leaves and flowers into the air. It's among the most ancient ways of Witchcraft.

The Witch stands in the center of the Greenwood magic, holding the mortar and pestle that wields the green forces. Here, they are gathered, shaped, and blended by the Witch and then released into the world by rite and by spell. At her or his side are the spirits that dwell within the Green Realm. They are the allies and companions of all who venerate the verdant places.

Plants, by nature, beneath the sun and moon are transformers of light. In their green blood, they hold the mysteries of the magical essence of light. This esoteric sentience is passed to their seeds and therefore to each generation. This is one of the reasons why cakes became part of ritual in occult circles. The grain from which cakes are made has gone into the soil as seeds. These seeds were steeped in the Underworld forces beneath the land, and then as plants they rose up into the world of light. They bring with them the knowledge of that which is below while gathering to themselves the knowledge of that which is above in the light. In the middle world of mortal-kind, they offer up all the inner mysteries to those who realize this truth.

In Greenwood magic, plants are under the domain of She of the White Round due to the esoteric connection between the phases of the moon and plant growth. Even among people outside of the magical community, the new and first-quarter phases are considered good for planting above-ground crops, grafting trees, and transplanting. The second-quarter moon, from half moon to full, is good for planting plants that bear vines, fruit, or grain. The third quarter, from full moon to half, is good for planting plants that have roots intended for magical and ritual usage.

The esoteric element associated with the moon and plants is intimately linked to the Night. At this time, plants are typically still and receptive, as is the dreamer. Visions and experiences are unhindered by the practicalities of the conscious mind, and therefore all things become possible in the late hours of the night watch. It's for this reason that the Witch calls upon She of the White Round prior to performing any work of magic:

> "She of the White Round, who commands silence when secret mysteries are performed, I invoke you.
>
> Night, faithful keeper of my secrets, and stars who, together with the moon, follow on from the fires of the daylight, I invoke you.
>
> Daughters of Night, the three faces, who know all my designs, and come to help the incantations and the Craft of the Witches, I invoke you.
>
> Earth, who furnishes Witches with powerful herbs, and you, Breezes, Winds, Mountains, Rivers, and Lakes, and all the gods of the groves and all the gods of the Night, be present to help me.

Night-wandering Queen, and Lord of the Deep Wooded Places, I invoke you.

I bid all to look kindly now upon this undertaking."

Any work of magic can now be performed. You may want to set a ritual or magical circle in place before performing a magical work. This allows the energy to collect without portions of it slipping away until you are ready to release it. A cohesive and condensed sphere of energy serves to hold your magical intent. In the Thorn Path of Witchery, this is called Setting the Round and is related to the idea of casting of a circle in modern Wicca and Witchcraft systems.

The Round is sensed as an enclosure (visualization isn't a preferred method over sensing, for the latter gives tangibility, and memory recall is best in terms of *being there*). The core concept of the Round is rooted in the vision of being in the deep woods surrounded by trees and lush foliage. Overhead is the vast canopy of leafy tree branches that mark the boundary of above. Beneath stretches the network of entangled roots. Surrounding is the wall of thorny hedges. This is a place of sanctuary and of sacred space. In keeping with the Thorn Path imagery, it's also a barrier against any intruder. The thorny hedges guard you all around, the canopy deflects, and the entwined roots make the way in impassible. The formal method of Setting the Round is provided in chapter 9, "The Modern Solitary Rites."

Magic is an essence in addition to an art in Old World Witchcraft. The art is about how to draw it, collect it, and make it something cohesive. The concept of an enclosed ritual space relates to shaping the essence of magic so that it can be impregnated with a magical intention (meaning the goal of the spell or ritual). The essence of magic emanates from all things. We can envision this as a mist. The emanation is raw energy; it has no intention imprinted within it. In the art of magic, we transmit our intention into the gathered essence, and we create a vehicle through which we direct the manifestation of our desire. This target can be a person, place, thing, or even situation.

Some people define magic as the art of manifesting what is desired, and indeed this is the mechanism; but magic is also a state of being, a thing in and of itself.

You may have heard the term *Old Magic* as a distinction between past and present forms. We can even think of it to mean something old-school in nature. In the Thorn Path, the old ways of magic are linked to the natural realm of plants, minerals, and animals. It also embraces spirits that are associated with them. This is the source of magic, the generated energies emanating from different forms in Nature. However, we cannot fail to include the celestial powers of the sun, moon, and stars. The latter is often linked to talismans or amulets in order to place them "into the hands" as opposed to thinking of them above and far away. Magic, in Old World Witchcraft, isn't something intellectual or philosophical. It's not a belief—it's experienced.

THE MAGICAL CONNECTION OF ALL THINGS

In occult philosophy, we find the tenet that an inseparable connection exists between an object and what is chosen to represent it. Here we see that symbolism is linked to the nature of what it signifies. In this light, we can say that a piece of paper is linked to the plant realm from which it was produced. In this same way, the symbol of a plant spirit is connected to the spirit itself. This is similar to the old ideas that possessing a lock of someone's hair, or fingernail clippings, allows that person to be influenced in a spell. This is also the essential concept behind the voodoo doll and how it works.

In older forms of magic, we find the concept of mimicking something in order to draw it to us. In primitive forms of magic, this can be the sprinkling of water in the hopes of making rain, or the drawing of a herd to attract animals for food. This idea is also reliant upon the idea that *something* is listening, caring, responding (and perhaps even directing). For some people, this may be spirits or deities. For the atheist, it's a simple cause-and-effect relationship; it's merely energy relays or ripples.

Another aspect to consider is tied to the concept of as above, so below—which means that for everything physical, there's a non-material counterpart. In magic, this can mean that we have the light of the moon in our earthly existence and we have the ethereal energy of the moon in our rituals and works of magic. This is the idea of material and nonmaterial reality.

In Greenwood magic, the belief is that spirits inhabit physical plants in the same way that souls inhabit flesh bodies. The two are separate and yet function together to create a being. Just as a rein-carnating spirit may be drawn to dwell within a certain body (and life environment) so, too, is a plant spirit attracted to a specific type of plant. The love of growing plants that have no food value may be tied to a spiritual relationship with them. This can even be without a conscious awareness of it. Perhaps the person feels that he simply loves the beauty of the plant. It doesn't occur to him that beauty is part of the relationship, part of an exchange between two beings (humankind and plant-kind).

In Old World Witchcraft, we believe that plants communicate and do so through the aid of spirits. The *voices* of plants are carried in the wind, which means through chemicals from the leaves and flow-ers. This is one of the reasons why Witches of the Rose and Thorn Path *inhale* the plant spirit into their inner being through the scent of the plant or its blossom. Once joined in this way with the plant spirit, communication is greatly enhanced through interfacing.

Plants and their spirits communicate with each other not only on the wind but also through the network of roots beneath the soil. These roots are believed to allow information that's contained in the organic memory of the earth to be transmitted through the plant's conscious spirit. Several decades ago, the popular term for this was *to hear the voice of the wind*, which meant being taught by spirits or through something Otherworldly.

All of this is tied to the occult belief that everything is connected together whether or not it exists in the same dimension. Magic doesn't travel from spell caster to target; it emerges within it. Everything reacts simultaneously. Connected to this concept is the axiom that like attracts like, which means that things of the same nature are pulled together into an interactive relationship. This relationship is greater than the general connection between all things. It's heightened and focused. One example is the affirmation of statements of well-being, which affirm health. To maintain positive thoughts is to exist in the current of their vibration.

In magic use, you can place symbols in your environment that represent what you wish to enhance in your life. For example, by placing symbols of prosperity in your home, you can attract it into your life. Seeing them each day reinforces the flow of the current to you and your life. However, the opposite is true as well, and if you always speak to your lack, you will continue to manifest it in your life. The Universe is listening, and your thoughts can and do become things in your life.

Another important aspect of connection is the concept of building a rapport with something. For example, if we say, "In the name of the Goddess," but we spend very little time connecting with her or venerating her, how powerful is that statement coming from us? If it's weak in us, it's a weak connection to her. In this same light, if we say, "As my word, so mote it be," but our word isn't our bond, what power are we bringing? It's the same with saying, "As my will, so mote it be"—if our will to accomplish something is weak, then we're calling upon weakness to empower our rituals or spells.

In order for our magic to be sound, we must be as well. This is why the customary training of a Witch involves strengthening the will, working on mental and emotional discipline, and being reliable to ourselves and to others. If a Witch gives her or his word of honor, there should be no doubt that it holds true and sees its way to the end. That's where the Witch wields personal power.

GREENWOOD MAGIC

As previously noted, the Greenwood magic is connected to various spirits that inhabit the plants of Witchcraft. This ancient connection between plants and Witches is deeply rooted in the Old Magic. In the spiritual perspective of the Rose and Thorn Path the organic memory of the earth (Shadow) holds the memory of the Witch as the Pharmakeute. This is the nature of the Witch as one with an intimate connection to the plants and their spirits. It's the memory of the Witch as one who honors the plant realm and venerates the spirits that inhabit it.

As a whole, humans have a negative reputation within the plant realm. We are regarded as "the termite people," chewing up everything in our path. This is one reason why it's important to awaken the ancient memory of the Pharmakeute so that the Greenwood recalls those who once embraced a spiritual relationship. This is accomplished through the exchange of the red and the green blood and by the announcement of connection.

To begin, find an area that's conducive to making contact with the plant world without being disturbed by other people. Go to the largest tree at the site. You will be making a connection with Shadow (organic memory of the earth) through the deep roots of the tree. All that's required is a container of fresh water, some liquid chlorophyll, three coins of your choosing, and a needle or thorn for pricking your finger.

Begin by approaching the tree slowly. Kneel near the base of its trunk. Place the palms of both hands on the ground, and then focus your thoughts on your love of plant life. Use your breath to send this sentiment to the leaves of the tree. Exhale three times in this manner. You are communicating on the wind as trees do.

The next phase is to place the container of water in front of the tree. Pour a small amount of chlorophyll (the green blood) into the water, and then prick your finger and squeeze out three drops of blood. Mix this in with the green blood. Pour some of the mixture out on the base of the trunk where it meets the ground. Rise to your feet, and then spread your arms and legs out to form an *X* posture. It's then time to speak the words of awakening memory:

> "Hear me, I am Pharmakeute!
> Shadow below, remember my kind,
> Roots, draw up the ancient memory,
> Trunk, fix and bind our blood oath,
> Branches proclaim to the wooded places
> That the Witch is joined to the Greenwood once again!"

Lift up the container of water and drink a small portion, and then say:

> "We are one through the blood,
> We are one in the voice of the wind,
> We are one through the Spirit of the Land."

All that remains now is to sit against the tree with the base of your spine pressed comfortably against the base of the tree trunk. Sense that you are a tree with roots extending down into the earth. Sit receptively and wait for communication on some level. Do not force it—just be open to receiving it. After a few minutes, you can rise and leave the area. Leave an offering of coins pressed into the soil.

In the future, whenever you want to connect to the Greenwood and its magic, simply take up the *X* posture (holding your wand in your left hand) and make the declaration to summon:

> "I am Pharmakeute,
> Roots beneath, hear me,
> Shadow below, know me.
> Branches above, connect me,
> For in-between I stand
> As a Thorn-Blooded Witch of the Ways."

This will rouse the consciousness of the Greenwood and connect you to it in mind, body, and spirit. The wand is the direct link to the plant world, and it draws the spirits of the Green Realm to you. Through its presence, the spirits look upon you with favor. To bring them into your service, hold your wand upright in your right hand and then kneel to lower it to touch the ground. Next, place your left hand upon the ground, point the wand outward away from you, and then call to the Greenwood spirits of the place:

"I summon the green spirits of this place."

Inhale slowly and deeply, and then release your breath toward any foliage. Then continue summoning:

"Come to the Thorn-Blooded Witch who hails,
I call you to pass through the verdant veils.
I reach out from the time-honored power,
By seed, sprout, budded-leaf and flower."

This method is good when you don't want to isolate any particular plant spirit to work with but instead want to draw the collective spirit of the Greenwood beings.

When working with plant spirits, it's important to remember that these aren't tame beings. They're also not personal servants. It's wise to regard them as allies and to keep in good standing with them. Working with plant spirits is sometimes called riding them. A fragmented memory of this resides in old folkloric images of Witches riding on twigs and later on brooms. To ride is to harness the energy and be propelled to reach altered states of consciousness. One of the risks of working with plant spirits is that they may try and ride you instead of being ridden. Relationships with plant spirits are always two sided. Give them a reason to be favorable to you, and they will be; give them a reason to use you, and they will. The latter isn't wise.

SAFELY WORKING WITH PLANT SPIRITS

There are three important elements to working safely with plant spirits:

- Offerings
- Rapport with She of the Thorn-Blooded Rose
- Plant seals

Offerings are like giving small gifts to friends. It's an endearing act. Maintaining rapport with She of the Thorn-Blooded Rose is important because she has great influence over plant spirits. As your ally, she will aid you as need be, and you can and should call upon her. Lastly, plant seals control connection and relationship with plant spirits. The seals can summon the spirits to you as well as release them from you.

The traditional plants of Witchcraft are often called baneful, which means "poisonous or harmful." In reality, that's not the purpose of the plant's existence on earth. In other words, these plants are simply part of the diversity of plant life on the earth. They don't exist for the purpose of poisoning other life forms; they're here to fulfill the role of being a plant, as is true of all in the Green Realm. It's the interaction with a plant that determines the experience.

When I work with plants possessing baneful properties, I use gloves and take great care not to touch my eyes and mouth during my direct encounters. Likewise, when working with plant spirits, I use seals. It's not only a practical concern; it's a show of respect for their potency. Nothing will put you into harm's way more profoundly than disrespect and arrogance. While the Witch is one who works in the so-called supernatural realm, she or he's not immune to the laws of Nature in the material world.

One empowering thought is to realize that we're not alone on the path of magic. We're accompanied, companioned, and protected when we're true to the Ways. The entity known as She of the Thorn-Blooded Rose is a great strength for the Witch. She's the living connection between the Witch and the spirits of Witchcraft in the Greenwood. Spend time building and maintaining a rapport with her. If there's a Witch in the consciousness of Nature, it's She of the Thorn-Blooded Rose.

Using the plant seals in Greenwood magic will prove to be empowering to you in the magical arts of Witchcraft. They can be drawn on parchment or on wooden disks (anything from the plant realm). You can use the relatively elaborate methods of summoning plant spirits as outlined in chapter 4, or you can use a simpler method once you have a good feel for working with these spirits. One method involves using a white plate and some garden soil.

Begin by covering the plate with a thin layer of soil. Using a finger, draw a large triangle in the soil (it needs to take up most of the plate). Next, inside the triangle, draw the seal of the plant spirit in the soil (the white of the plate should show as you draw). Then place the palm of your left hand down over the seal, hold a single red rose in your right hand, and call the spirit using its name:

> "_____, spirit of the plant called _____, I summon you in the name of She of the Thorn-Blooded Rose, and in the memory of all the Pharmakeute from days of old."

Place the rose in a container of water, as this will give the spirit a plant form to anchor to for the remainder of the work. You can then make your request to the spirit. Ask it to perform a specific task, and then give a detailed description of what you want to manifest. Leave the rose in place for three days, and save the plate for use at that time (do not remove or disturb the soil).

On the third day, remove the rose from its container and hover the blossom directly over the center of the plate. Call the spirit using its name. Then inform it that you are releasing it back into its natural dwelling place, and give thanks for its aid. Finish by setting the blossom on the center of the plate, and then erase the seal image by dragging the rose through the soil in a counterclockwise motion. Once this is done, erase anything that remains of the triangle imprint. As you work with the blossom, make a verbal affirmation that you're releasing the spirit back to its natural place.

To complete this work of magic, take the plate outside and toss the soil into the air (making sure that any wind is coming from behind you). Then blow your breath across the surface of the plate, and say:

> "I release into the air the spell of the Green,
> Here, and there, and in-between.
> Spirits fly and take no rest
> Until my wish is manifest."

The spell is now fully cast, and you can clean up any debris. Return the rose to the container of water. As it withers, this is recognition that the magic is being drawn into the intended purpose. Keep the rose until it withers completely. Afterward, bury it outside in the earth.

On rare occasions, you may find that a plant spirit has become unruly. In such cases, you must return it back to a harmonious relationship. The first step is to call upon She of the Thorn-Blooded Rose for intervention. Begin by obtaining three long-stemmed red roses. Remove all the petals and place them in a bowl of water. Next, draw the seal of She of the Thorn-Blooded Rose on a piece of paper and lay it in front of the bowl. Then place the palm of your left hand over the seal and evoke her:

> "I call now to She of the Thorn-Blooded Rose,
> To you all the mysteries of the Greenwood flows.
> Thorn bearer, Queen with the red-crowned flower,
> Come to my aid with your presence and power."

Lay the three stems down together to form a triangle. Then place the seal of the plant spirit inside the center of the triangle. Hold the seal of She of the Thorn-Blooded Rose in your left hand and place the palm of your left hand over the seal inside the triangle. Now, you can begin the work of quelling the unruly spirit. Begin by addressing She of the Thorn-Blooded Rose:

"My Lady of the Greenwood Realm, there's disharmony between myself and this spirit. I ask for your intervention to bring peace and cooperation."

Now, give an offering of liquid chlorophyll to the plant spirit and say:

"I wish peace between us, I give you this offering, and I ask that you overlook whatever caused disharmony between us. I ask this in the covenant between Witch and spirit, and in the name of She of the Thorn-Blooded Rose."

Wait a few minutes and sit quietly. When you feel the time is right, perform the following. Open the triangle of rose stems, pick up the plant seal, and lay it on top of the rose petals in the bowl of water. Next, pick up the seal of She of the Thorn-Blooded Rose in your left hand and hold it over the bowl, saying:

"I ask you to quell the spirit whose seal lies nested in your petals. Receive it back into your influence, and restore the feelings of cooperative partnership between us."

Next, gently place your finger on the plant spirit seal and say:

"Go now into the arms of She of the Thorn-Blooded Rose and be refreshed."

Push the seal down into the water so that the petals cover it, swish your finger in the water to release the seal from your touch, and then quickly pull your hand up out of the water. If the seal can still be seen, move some petals over it to remove it from your sight. Finish by giving thanks and bidding partings:

"I give thanks to you, She of the Thorn-Blooded Rose, and to you, the spirit of [name plant]. May there always be good will between us."

Leave everything in place for twenty-four hours.

MORTAR AND PESTLE MAGIC

The primary tool for working with plants and their spirits is the mortar and pestle set. The mortar is used to contain the material connections to various plants and for merging with the forces required for Greenwood Magic. The latter is incorporated through working in conjunction with the waxing and waning times of the earth tides and the moon. In accord with these elements, the pestle is stirred inside the mortar in the corresponding clockwise or counterclockwise direction.

For casting spells, the various parts of a plant are assigned magical properties. One or more of them can be used in a single spell. The list shows each part and its correspondence:

1. Flower: Represents the spirit of a matter or something of a spiritual nature

2. Bud: Represents potentiality and new ventures or ideas

3. Leaf: Represents energy, force, or power

4. Stem: Represents growth and expansion

5. Crown: Represents transition

6. Root: Represents foundation and vitalization

7. Seed: Represents preservation and renewal

To begin spell casting with the mortar and pestle, think about the intent of the spell. What links to the desired effects do you need to bring into play? What will propel the spell?

This is where you review the list of plant parts and select which ones will enhance the spell. In other words what does the intent of the spell require? Is it energy, expansion, or transition? What part best serves the spell? Think about the symbolism and then add the part or parts of the plant to the mortar. In most cases, you'll choose two or more parts of the plant. Do not, however, remove so much that you end up killing the plant.

The following sample spell can be modified for any intent and will help you better understand spell casting with this tool. Let's look at a healing spell designed to help someone recover from illness or surgery.

To Heal with Mortar and Pestle

Begin by placing the mortar in the east quarter. Fill it one-quarter full with fresh water, saying:

> "Here is the cleansing water that purifies and heals as it now enters the sacred womb."

Next, say:

> "I call to the spirits of the Greenwood."

Then tap the mortar with the pestle three times. Immediately after this, give the evocation:

> "Come to the Thorn-Blooded Witch who hails,
> I call you to pass through the verdant veils.
> I reach out from the time-honored power,
> By seed, sprout, budded leaf, and flower."

Place both palms over the mortar and say:

> "Spirits of the Greenwood, I ask for your aid in this spell of healing."

Now, drop three flower petals into the mortar and say:

> "Spirit, fill this potion with uplifting life force."

Drop three leaves into the mortar and say:

> "Energy rise and quicken the healing."

Drop three seeds into the mortar and say:

> "Renewal awakens and refreshes health in body, mind, and spirit."

Pick up the pestle and insert the tip into the opening of the mortar. Begin rotating the pestle in a clockwise motion, saying:

> "Turn the Wheel
> Set the task
> Bring about
> The thing I ask."

Repeat the above words three times, and then state the intention:

> "I work on behalf of [person's name] that her/his body quicken the healing process and return to full health once again in body, mind, and spirit."

Now, repeat the words of enchantment three more times:

> "Turn the Wheel
> Set the task
> Bring about
> The thing I ask."

Finish by placing all of the contents of the mortar into a pan. Fill it about half full with fresh water. Place the pan over fire until the water boils. Allow this to simmer for about five minutes, and then strain the liquid. Pour the filtered liquid into a bottle or jar with a lid. Keep it sealed until time to use it.

End by releasing the spirits to return to the Greenwood Realm:

> "Spirits of the Greenwood, I thank you for your presence, and as you depart, I ask that you bestow your blessings upon this potion."

When you are ready to send the healing, there are several methods of delivery. One method is to add the potion to some water inside a vase of flowers and then deliver them to the person in recovery. Another way is to anoint a piece of jewelry that's given to the person. For long-distance healing, boil the potion in a pan and blow the rising steam in the direction of the person (enhance this by using a photo as a link). Add these words of enchantment whenever activating the spell's potion:

> "I send the Greenwood magic, ever renewing, ever growing.
> I give you the healing water that's the essence of Nature itself."

To Quell with Mortar and Pestle

The purpose of this spell is to calm and dissolve away conflicts and disharmony. For this spell, you will use only rose flowers and a piece of root. Set your mortar and pestle in front of you with three roses. Next, pick up the pestle, rap it three times on the mortar, and say:

> "I call to the spirits of the Greenwood."

Now, pick up one of the roses and circle it over the opening of the mortar, saying:

> "Come to the Thorn-Blooded Witch who hails,
> I call you to pass through the verdant veils.
> I reach out from the time-honored power,
> By seed, sprout, budded leaf, and flower."

Place both palms over the mortar and say:

> "Spirits of the Greenwood, I ask for your aid in this spell of quelling."

Fill the mortar about half full with fresh water, saying:

> "I pour the calming and cleansing water into the womb that births peace."

Name two of the roses after the people in conflict (both sides are symbolized) and lay them inside the mortar. Say:

"I bathe you in the water that dispels all disharmony."

Then take the pestle, circle it over the mortar, and say:

"Around you now I weave a spell, and sound the heart's pure lulling bell."

Rap the pestle against the inside of the mortar to mimic the sound of a heartbeat. Do this in three sets of two beats. Then slowly turn the pestle clockwise against the inside rim of the mortar, and continue with the words of enchantment:

"To these spirits of unrest, the quelling spirit I do send."

Reverse the motion of the pestle, saying:

"I spin all hearts a peace, and the rift I do now mend" (repeat this three times).

Now, hold both palms over the mortar and say:

"Spirits of the Greenwood, I ask for your aid in quelling any disharmony and ill will between [give names]. Send forth the evergreen forces of renewal, and restore the bonds between those who have set themselves against each other."

End by releasing the spirits to return to the Greenwood Realm:

"Spirits of the Greenwood, I thank you for your presence, and as you depart, I ask that you bestow your blessings upon this spell."

Conclude the work by tying the roses together. If possible, place them somewhere in a setting that one or both of the parties will be in at some point. The alternative is to put the roses in flowing water (such as a stream or river). You can also use the ocean tides.

To Bind with Mortar and Pestle

This is a general spell designed to quell ill intentions and actions directed against you or someone you know. To begin, establish a link to the person who needs to be bound from doing harm. This can be a photo, a personal object that came into contact with her, or the person's name on a piece of parchment. Put the link inside the mortar and wrap some ivy or another type of vine around it.

Next, say:

"I call to the spirits of the vine within the Greenwood."

Then tap the mortar with the pestle three times. Immediately after this, give the evocation:

"Come to the Thorn-Blooded Witch who hails,
I call you to pass through the verdant veils.
I reach out from the time-honored power,
By seed, sprout, budded leaf, and flower."

Place both palms over the mortar and say:

"Spirits of the Greenwood vines, I ask for your aid in this spell of binding."

Next, begin tapping the pestle back and forth inside the mortar. Do this in a metered beat, like the sound of an old clock or the beat of a heart. Use the pestle to keep a slow and deliberate, steady meter as you give the incantation, your words in time with the beat:

"Mark the spirit,
Set the time.
[man/woman] named _____ I here now bind.
No wagging tongue,
No rolling eyes,
No harmful acts,
No more your lies.

Wag your tongue—your throat grows sore.
Roll your eyes—a headache roars.
Harm someone—you grow forlorn.
Spread your lies—you fall on thorns."

Repeat the incantation several times. Your goal is to get your emotions roused to create energy. Keep your mind focused on the mental image of the person. When you feel ready to stop, remove the pestle quickly and rap it three times on the rim of the mortar, proclaiming:

"[Name of person], I bind you so!"

Now, hold both palms over the mortar and say:

"Spirits of the Greenwood, I ask for your aid in binding this person from harming anyone in mind, body, or spirit. Send forth the evergreen forces to entangle, ensnare, and hold fast in the thickets."

End by releasing the spirits to return to the Greenwood Realm:

"Spirits of the Greenwood, I thank you for your presence, and as you depart, I ask that you bestow your favor upon this spell."

Take the link and the vine out of the mortar and place them in a pouch. Fasten the pouch closed and put it in your freezer. You can undo the binding by taking the items out of the pouch (during a waning moon), cutting the vine in half, and then destroying the link with fire. Bury any ashes with the vine.

THE STAR PENTACLES

The use of magical pentacles is often associated with the arts of Witchcraft. In the Rose and Thorn Path, we assign them largely to celestial magic. The idea behind them is about using symbolism to draw the influences of stars or planets (and to some, this is the calling upon spirits of the outer spaces). Each pentacle contains the seal that connects the symbolism with the forces they represent, and it is drawn at a specific time of day and on a particular day of the week. This is because occult forces are linked to such things.

The pentacles bear the five-pointed star symbol, which represents the elemental forces of creation and the stars from which we all come. In Old World Witchcraft, the five-pointed star in a circle symbolizes the moon impregnated with the star-seed, the enlightener who descends into the mortal realm to liberate humankind. This adds a mystical element to the symbolism of the pentacles and can be regarded as receiving aid from star-beings (a somewhat related theme reflected in the old tale of the watchers who taught the "forbidden arts" to humans).

The basic system of pentacles consists of seven planetary seals: Moon, Sun, Venus, Mars, Mercury, Jupiter, and Saturn. This system is sometimes called the Magic of the Wanderers. Celestial magic is arguably among the oldest forms of the arts in Witchcraft and is still honored within the contemporary practice of Old World Witchcraft.

Pentacle of the Moon

This celestial influence aids in psychic matters, dream control, summoning and directing lunar forces of magic, and calming the tides of emotion. It can also be helpful in aiding fertility. The seal is drawn upon white paper beginning at nine p.m. During this process, three white candles are burning, along with an incense of the moon (jasmine scent). Once the pentacle is completed, it's then passed three times through the incense smoke.

Pentacle of the Sun

This pentacle aids in matters of daily life, relationships, careers, and social settings. The seal is drawn at noon on a Sunday. Light three yellow candles during the process and burn an incense of the sun (cinnamon scent). Once the pentacle is completed, it's then passed three times through the incense smoke.

Pentacle of Venus

This pentacle aids in matters of love, beautification, attraction, and intimate relationships of all kinds. It also has influence over plant spirits when working with Greenwood magic. The seal is drawn on a Friday at the beginning of the hour of three or seven (a.m. or p.m.).

Light three pink candles during the process and burn an incense of Venus (rose scent). Once the pentacle is completed, it's then passed three times through the incense smoke.

Pentacle of Mars

This pentacle gives aid to anyone in conflict, combat, trouble, or any dangerous situation. The seal is drawn on a Tuesday at 5 a.m. or 5 p.m.

Light three red candles during the process and burn an incense of Mars (tobacco scent). Once the pentacle is completed, it's then passed three times through the incense smoke.

Pentacle of Mercury

This pentacle aids in matters of communication, trade, commerce, and travel of any kind. It can also be used in matters of health. The seal is drawn at the beginning of any even-numbered hour of the day. Light three yellow candles during the process and burn an incense of Mercury (frankincense scent). Once the pentacle is completed, it's then passed three times through the incense smoke.

Pentacle of Jupiter

This pentacle aids in matters of prosperity, success, victory, and worldly recognition. This seal is drawn on a Thursday at the beginning of any even-numbered hour of the day or night. Light three orange candles during the process and burn an incense of Jupiter (clove scent). Once the pentacle is completed, it's then passed three times through the incense smoke.

Pentacle of Saturn

This pentacle aids in binding, limiting, constricting, and quelling. The seal is drawn on a Saturday at any hour of the day or night. Light three black candles during the process and burn an incense of Saturn (myrrh scent). Once the pentacle is completed, it's then passed three times through the incense smoke.

USING THE PENTACLES

A simple rite is used to empower the pentacles. It includes the use of a triangular image upon which the seals are placed, along with other items. The assembly becomes a focal point where magical energy can be condensed and empowered with a specific intent.

The use of the triangle for casting spells requires a colored candle, the root or leaves of a specific plant, and some anointing oil. You can purchase a general blessing oil for this purpose or make your own. For the latter, you can place some rosemary in a small pan of olive oil and heat to simmer on the stove for five minutes (do not boil). Afterward, strain the oil and allow it to cool.

On the day or night that corresponds to your magical intention, prepare the star pentacle as previously prescribed. I recommend that you use a heavy paper such as card stock. Set the triangle image on your work area (make sure your reproduction of it's large enough for the items to fit on it). Place the pentacle seal in the middle of the triangle, the candle in the top circle, the plant substance in the bottom left circle, and the oil in the bottom right circle.

The following spells are specific to a single intent but can be modified for manifesting other needs or desires. Think of them as models or formulas, and then make changes to the words as makes sense for your purpose.

Lunar

Draw down the light of the moon to enhance psychic abilities and reveal hidden mysteries.

Perform this on a Monday night at nine p.m. or midnight when the moon is waning. To begin, set the triangle sheet on your work area with the tip of the triangle pointing away from you. In the center of the triangle, place the pentacle seal between the three circles.

In the top circle, place the candle. In the bottom left circle, place the herb root. In the bottom right circle, place the vial of oil. Then light the candle and say:

"To me I draw the light of the moon."

Looking at the symbol of the moon on the seal, trace the star with your index finger (not touching it) and give the evocation:

"I call you, Pa-ee-oh, the spirit of the moon who aids in all spells cast beneath the moon. Come now in the name of She of the White Round who governs the night sky when the moon is full. Come, Pa-ee-oh, come to the call and aid me in my spell."

Next, raise your arms up and outward (form them to resemble a chalice). Then look upon the pentacle seal and say the following words:

"I am the open chalice, my life is the open chalice, my spirit's the open chalice."

Anoint the back of your left hand with the oil. Then, while holding your left hand so that you can take in the scent of the oil, use the index finger of the other hand to touch each point of the five-pointed star (moving clockwise from the top point). As you touch each point, say:

> "I am the chalice. I receive the power and aid of the spirit of the moon. I receive the mystical powers of the moon."

Place the oil and the plant material on top of the pentacle seal. Pick up the candle and move it clockwise over each of the circles on the triangle. As do you, say these words:

> "Pa-ee-oh, spirit of the moon, lend your aid as the light of the moon descends. Empower these objects to enhance psychic ability and to emanate the magical essence of the moon, whereby all mysteries are revealed in mystical light."

Gather up the seal and plant material, and place them in a carrying pouch. Extinguish the candle, remove the triangle paper, and clean up any debris. You should place the pouch with the items under your pillow when you go to bed (for the first three nights). Have the pouch with you when working with divination or seeking to reveal what is hidden from you. Look to dreams for the answers.

Solar

Attract the forces of the sun for success and good fortune.

Perform this on a Sunday morning at either sunrise or noon. The most favorable period is from the Spring Equinox to the Summer Solstice. Set the triangle sheet on your work area (with the tip of the triangle pointing away from you). In the center of the triangle, place the pentacle seal of the sun between the three circles.

In the top circle, place the candle. In the bottom left circle, place the herb root. In the bottom right circle, place the vial of oil. Then light the candle and say:

> "To me I draw the light of the sun."

Looking at the seal, trace the star with your index finger (not touching it) and give the evocation:

> "I call you, Pa-ray-ee, the spirit of the sun who aids in all spells cast beneath the sun. Come now in the name of the Great Horned One of Light who governs the day sky when the sun rules the heavens. Come, Pa-ray-ee, come to the call and aid me in my spell."

Next, place both palms of your hands facing down, and then touch your index fingers together and your thumbs together. If done correctly, your fingers should form a triangle. Bring the triangle up to the center of your forehead and say the following words:

> "I am the open mind, my life is the open opportunity, my spirit's the open way."

Anoint the back of your left hand with the oil. Then, while holding your left hand so that you can take in the scent of the oil, use the index finger of the other hand to touch each point of the five-pointed star (moving clockwise from the top point). As you touch each point, say:

> "I am the conscious thought. I receive the power and aid of the spirit of the sun. I receive the mystical powers of the sun."

Place the oil and the herb root on top of the talisman. Pick up the candle and move it clockwise over each of the circles on the triangle. As you do, say these words:

> "Pa-rey-ee, spirit of the sun, lend your aid as the light of the sun descends. Empower these objects to ensure my success and victory and to emanate the magical essence of the sun, whereby all worldly affairs prosper in life."

Gather up the seal and plant material, and place them in a carrying pouch. Extinguish the candle, remove the triangle paper, and clean up any debris. You should place the pouch with the items under your pillow when you go to bed (for the first three nights). Have the pouch with you when working on plans and projects and when participating in career, competition, goals, and aspirations.

Venus

Attract loving relationships that are ideal, beneficial, and enriching.

Perform this on a Friday evening at seven p.m. Set the triangle sheet on your work area (with the tip of the triangle pointing away from you). In the center of the triangle, place the pentacle of Venus between the three circles.

In the top circle, place the candle. In the bottom left circle, place the plant material. In the bottom right circle, place the vial of oil. Then light the candle and say:

"To me I draw the light of Venus."

Looking at the star symbol, trace it with your index finger (not touching it) and give the evocation:

"I call you, Suroth, the spirit of Venus who aids in all spells cast beneath the star. Come now in the name of She who is jeweled in stars, she who governs the stellar realm of the celestial heavens. Come, Suroth, come to the call and aid me in my spell."

Next, cross your wrists over your heart area, hands flat and fingers spread. Envision them as wings, and then say the following words:

"I am the open wings, my life is the lifting breeze, my spirit's the eye in the sky."

Anoint the back of your left hand with the oil. Then, while holding your left hand so that you can take in the scent of the oil, use the index finger of the other hand to touch each point of the five-pointed star (moving clockwise from the top point). As you touch each point, say:

"I am the faithful flight. I receive the power and aid of the spirit of Venus. I receive the mystical powers of Venus."

Place the oil and the plant material on top of the pentacle seal. Pick up the candle and move it clockwise over each of the circles on the triangle. As do you, say these words:

"Suroth, spirit of Venus, lend your aid as the light of the stars shines from above. Empower these objects to ensure my match with the perfect (man/woman), to draw us together soon. Suroth, emanate the magical essence of Venus whereby kindred hearts are united in love."

Gather up the seal and plant material, and place them in a carrying pouch. Extinguish the candle, remove the triangle paper, and clean up any debris. You should place the pouch with the items under your pillow when you go to bed (for the first three nights). Have the pouch with you when going out into social environments, on dates, or wherever there's any opportunity to meet someone new.

Mercury

Envelop yourself in magnetic energy to place yourself in the stream of prosperity and gain.

Perform this on a Wednesday any time during the daylight hours. Set the triangle sheet on your work area (with the tip of the triangle pointing away from you). In the center of the triangle, place the pentacle of Mercury between the three circles. Set a magnet with the seal.

In the top circle, place the candle. In the bottom left circle, place the herb root. In the bottom right circle, place the vial of oil. Then light the candle and say:

"To me I draw the emanation of prosperity."

Look at the pentacle image. Use both hands to form a triangle by touching the tips of each index finger and each thumb together. Position the hands so that you can see the seal of Mercury through the opening, and then give the evocation:

"I call you, O-phal-ah, the spirit of Mercury, the endless force of renewal, growth, and abundance. Come, spirit of Mercury, come to the call and aid me in my spell."

Next, place both palms together and then slowly open them. Looking at the image of the seal, say the following words:

"I am open to receive bounty, my life is open to abundance, my spirit's the essence of endless growth."

Anoint the back of your left hand with the oil. Then use the fingers of both hands again to form the triangle (hold your hands close enough to your nose so that you take in the scent of the oil). Next, look at the seal through the opening between your hands and say:

"I see the arrival of bounty. I receive the harvest of abundance. I am the filled basket of plenty."

Place the oil and the plant material on top of the talisman. Pick up the candle and move it clockwise over each of the circles on the triangle. As do you, say these words:

"Spirit of Mercury, lend your aid as the light falls to empower my spell. I call to you, O-Phal-ah, to empower these objects to attract financial gain, growth, success, and prosperity."

Gather up the seal, plant material, oil, and lodestone, and place them in a carrying pouch. Extinguish the candle, remove the triangle paper, and clean up any debris. You should place the pouch with the items under your pillow when you go to bed (for the first three nights). Have the pouch with you in work settings and any situation that involves finances or associated opportunities for additional income.

Mars

Surround yourself with a barrier of energy to prevent negative or harmful intentions from influencing body, mind, and spirit.

Perform this on a Thursday or Saturday night at seven p.m. or midnight. To begin, set the triangle sheet on your work area (with the tip of the triangle pointing away from you). In the center of the triangle, place the seal of Mars between the three circles.

In the top circle, place the candle. In the bottom left circle, place the herb root. In the bottom right circle, place the vial of oil. Then light the candle and say:

"To me I draw the forces that banish all darkness."

Looking at the symbol of the five-pointed star, trace the star with your index finger (not touching it) and give the evocation:

"I call to you, spirits of protection: Abdia, Ballaton, Bellony, Halliy, Halliza, and Soluzen, come and lend your aid to my spell."

Place the oil and the plant material on top of the talisman. Pick up the candle and move it clockwise over each of the circles on the triangle. As do you so, say these words:

"Here now the conquering spear of light descends, and in its presence darkness ends."

Next, return the items back to their original circle positions. Then look at the star image. Use both hands to form a triangle by touching the tips of your index fingers and thumbs together. Position the hands so that you can see the star through the opening, and then give the evocation:

"Strict charge and watch I give you, that to this place where you abide, no evil thing may approach or enter in. Strict charge and watch I give you, that to whoever bears your image, no evil thing may approach or enter in."

Gather up the seal and plant material, and place them in a carrying pouch. Extinguish the candle, remove the triangle paper, and clean up any debris. You should place the pouch with the items under your pillow when you go to bed (for the first three nights). Place the pouch in an area you wish to protect, or have it on your person when you feel you need protection.

Saturn

Bind the harmful actions of others.

Perform this on a Saturday evening at nine p.m. Set the triangle sheet on your work area (with the tip of the triangle pointing away from you). In the center of the triangle, place the pentacle of Saturn between the three circles.

In the top circle, place the candle. In the bottom left circle, place the plant material. In the bottom right circle, place the vial of oil. Then light the candle and say:

"To me I draw the light of Saturn."

Looking at the star symbol, trace it with your index finger (not touching it) and give the evocation:

"I call you, Araton, the spirit of Saturn who aids in all spells cast beneath the star. Come now in the name of She of the Crossroads who is veiled in the night, she who watches the paths we chose as witnessed by the stars. Come, Araton, come to the call and aid me in my spell."

Anoint the back of your left hand with the oil. Then, while holding your left hand so that you can take in the scent of the oil, use the index finger of the other hand to touch each point of the five-pointed star (moving clockwise from the top point). As you touch each point, say:

"I am the appointed trapper. I receive the power and aid of the spirit of Saturn. I receive the mystical powers of Saturn."

Place the oil and the plant material on top of the pentacle seal. Pick up the candle and move it clockwise over each of the circles on the triangle. As do you, say these words:

"Araton, spirit of Saturn, lend your aid as the light of the stars shines from above. Empower these objects to ensnare my enemies, to bind all who seek to harm me in mind, body, or spirit. Araton, emanate the magical essence of Saturn whereby cruel hearts and mean-spirited foes are stilled and silenced."

Next, trace a footprint in the soil with a sharp stick. If any names are known, etch them in the dirt inside the footprint. Next, hold the stick up like a dagger, pointing down at the image, and then say the following words:

"I am the staker, closer, and ender of all conflict."

Now, forcefully drive the sharp end of the stick down into the footprint, and then, while holding it in place, say these words:

"I bind you here, and you are unable to harm me or act against me. Your influence is driven into the earth and swallowed whole."

Push the stake all the way down into the soil. Then gather up the seal and plant material, and place them in a carrying pouch. Extinguish the candle, remove the triangle paper, and clean up any debris. You should place the pouch with the items under your pillow when you go to bed (for the first three nights). Have the pouch with you when you're in any setting that can result in contact with your enemy. This includes the internet.

6

THE OLD ONES

In some forms of old Witch lore, we find the belief in an elder race of beings. Some are obscure, while others appear as relatively clear concepts in contemporary Witchcraft. These include guardians, watchers, and rulers of the four elements of earth, air, fire, and water. In some systems of Witchcraft, we also find the Faery Race incorporated into modern practices and beliefs. There is, however, a more primal view of such beings associated with Witchcraft.

In Old World Witchcraft, we find the concept of Night as the most ancient of beings. Night is the mother of all that came to be on the earth. It's the corridor through which manifestation moves into fruition. Night is the conceptual mind, the birthing place of all that can be but has yet to take form. As ideas open in the Night like the buds of plants, they are shadowy images. A shadow cannot exist without light behind it, and so the shadowed places became indications of something generating them. The ancestral experience was that even in daylight, the deep places of the forest were filled with shadows. Some of our distant ancestors dared to cross the Shadow's Edge, and these were the forbearers of all Witches.

Within the deep forests in which our ancestors once lived, human experience was much different than the world we understand and experience today. As noted, the dense growth of the old forests created shadowy areas, hiding places, and barriers. Sounds arose in these places, but their source could not be seen. Spirits and various creatures were believed to inhabit the deep places of the forest. This gave rise to the tales of enchanted woods and a myriad race of unseen supernatural beings. Among the beings that could be encountered in the forest were the Faeries, but other creatures of the deep-wooded places walked the forest as well.

GODS IN THE WOODED PLACES

From the perspective of Old World Witchcraft, the idea of a formal goddess, god, or even spirit arose from something less defined. It was felt and experienced long before it was given a name or depicted in imagery. These are the Old Ones, the nameless and formless beings of a forgotten time. This isn't unlike the idea of the Di Involuti of the Etruscan pantheon, a race of beings that existed above the High Gods (and who were given no physical form or imagery). The Greek idea of the Titans, a primal race of deities, may also be a reflection of prehistoric ideas that endured even if only in the form of fragmented memories.

Classical writings from the ancient period include stories about Witches involved with deities. Medea calls upon Hecate, Canidia evokes Diana, and so on. Witches, just like other people in ancient times, knew about gods and goddesses. Ancient writings contain period beliefs that depict Witches evoking various types of deity in their rites and magical practices. In modern times, some people reject this theme and regard Witchcraft as simply a personal practice with no attachment to religious or spiritual concepts. However, this doesn't appear to match ancient thought.

The rooted concepts in the Rose and Thorn Path of Witchery are based upon the idea that our ancestors sensed something sentient and unseen in the world around them. The mountains, rivers, forests, and wetlands all possessed a mindful presence, one that could be persuaded to aid people if given appropriate enticement (most commonly through offerings). This is where the concept of He of the Deep Wooded Places arises, along with other beings within Old World Witchcraft. Among the most noted are She of the White Round, the Three Daughters of Night, and She of the Pathways (later to be known as She of the Crossroads).

He of the Deep Wooded Places can be viewed as the root origin of various god forms in modern Witchcraft and Wicca. Elements of him can certainly be separated out to reflect the Stag-Horned God and the Green Man so popular in contemporary Wicca and Witchcraft. Although in his oldest and truest nature, He of the Deep Wooded Places has no specific form, in modern times, he's occasionally depicted as a white stag. The color white is associated with the Otherworld, and the stag is regarded as the spirit of the forest (his antlers bearing a resemblance to tree branches). In this light, he's a primal god of the Witches and more about him will be discussed in chapter 7, "The Mythos." But for now, we can say that he's not the Creator of All Things but is instead a god associated with the untamed world and with the process through which souls enter and leave the mortal realm.

The Rose and Thorn Path of Witchery is aligned to both the terrestrial and the Celestial Realm. In the latter connection, we find an entity known as She of the White Round. This entity is the moon seen as living and self-aware. The moon was, no doubt, a thing of great mystery to our distant ancestors who knew nothing about objects in outer space, at least certainly not as we understand them today. It must have been easy to attach the concept of a mystical goddess to the moon in ancient times. When thought of as a goddess, She of the White Round is intimately connected with souls of the dead through her association with the realm of LuNeya, which is a term for the place in the lunar sphere where souls await rebirth.

Old World Witchcraft is, at its core, lunar oriented. Night and the shadowed places are sacred and powerful. The color black is also sacred because it represents the fullness of potentiality, which is reflected in the fact that black is the presence of all colors combined together. Black conceals all that it contains, and through this, it shields the sacred from the profane.

The Night is the time of the Witch because she or he receives the light of the moon, which is considered to be an Otherworld light as opposed to a worldly light. Sunlight reveals things as they are, while moonlight transforms things into what they can or might be. Walking terrain by moonlight calls for caution and discernment because things are not always what they seem. This is true also of the dreamscape when we sleep. The two realms are intimately connected.

The Realm of Dreams is intimately connected to the Three Daughters of Night. Within Witchcraft, the number three is mystical in nature. One of its attributes is manifestation (as in the symbol of the Triangle of Manifestation). In occult philosophy, three things are required in order for anything to become manifest: time, space, and energy. Within material reality this principle is rigid, while in the Dream Realm it's fluid and anything is possible to appear, shift, and transform without apparent order or conformity.

The Three Daughters of Night are, in essence, the keepers and the bearers of the inner mysteries. Their place in the Rose and Thorn Path is to connect the Witch to the mystical currents that empower magic and the Witches' Craft in general. This is accomplished through being linked to the Three Daughters on a personal level.

The Three Daughters of Night individually bear a symbol denoting their domain. The first sister is clothed in a black robe and holds a serpent. She's called the Lady of Shadow. Her formal name is Potia (poe-tee-ah), and she represents the occult principle of energy in terms of endless manifesting. The serpent, as a creature that descends beneath the earth and reappears again, symbolizes Potia's nature to absorb and re-form all things. In the Mysteries of birth, life, and death, she symbolizes the first concept, which is connected to the timeless question: where did we come from?

The second sister wears a red robe and holds a human heart, which opens as a rose blossom. She's known as the Lady of the Blood. Her formal name is Arrea (ar-ree-ah), and she signifies the occult principle of space in terms of what is central and finite. The heart represents the flow of the river of blood from one generation to the next. The blood that pumps through our veins and arteries carries the genetic memory, or organic memory, of all who came before us in our bloodline. In the Mysteries of birth, life, and death, Arrea symbolizes the second concept, which is connected to the timeless question: why are we here?

Timia (tim-ee-ah) is the third sister, and she wears a white robe. She's known as the Lady of Bone. In her hands is a human skull, which represents the life experience and what remains after death. This is known as the bone memory, and within it is held the essence of our very existence in the Material Realm. In the Mysteries of birth, life, and death, Timia symbolizes the third, which is connected to the timeless question: what happens to us after we die?

The Three Daughters are associated with the night for two reasons. One is because the night veils things, obscures them, and requires a more concentrated discernment. Night is also the most common time for sleep, and therefore for dreaming. In dreams, we encounter a realm that functions in seemingly magical ways, one in which anything can happen; anything is possible. This is the essence of the inner mysteries, and the Three Daughters of Night are its operatives. They are evoked in various rites and spell casting. They are particularly linked with rites of the dark moon when the moon is unseen for three nights. Further information is found in chapters 5 and 8, "Works of Magic" and "The Old Rites."

Another entity in Old World Witchery is known as She of the Crossroads. Some people identify her with the goddess Hecate. However, in the philosophy of the Rose and Thorn Path, to name a deity is to place a finite nature on it. Therefore, we prefer the use of descriptive titles. A name also connects a deity to a specific cultural depiction as well as to associated elements within any given culture. By contrast, a title is more expansive in terms of perception and comprehension. In this light, She of the Crossroads represents the complete concept of the crossroads, its function, nature, elements, and all that it connects to in Witchcraft. She's not a goddess that stands or waits at the crossroads; she's all that the crossroads mean and can be to the Witch. This is an important reason why she and other entities in Old World Witchcraft bear titles as opposed to names.

The use of titles is extended to what some people may call elemental spirits, watchers, or guardians of the Witches' ritual or magical circle. In the Rose and Thorn Path, we use the title Asthesia, which denotes the primal consciousness of the four elements of earth, air, fire, and water. This consciousness existed long before humans personified the elements, gave them names and visual images. In Old World Witchcraft, they are honored in their earliest forms, which preexisted us and first arose in the minds of our ancestors upon realizing such a thing existed. This wordless understanding was the initiatory moment linking humankind with the elemental natures.

The Asthesia are energies that work together to create and dissolve away all formations. They are evoked when Setting the Round (circle casting) in order to create the enclosure and protective boundary for rituals. Upon the completion of a rite, they are released. Their withdrawal dissolves away the energy that sustains cohesion, and in its absence, the circle dissipates and is released. In other words, the formed-idea of a ritual or magical circle (the Round) then evaporates, and the space returns to its former everyday status.

In terms of ritual representation, the Asthesia are symbolized by placing a bowl containing soil (north quarter), one containing three feathers (east quarter), another containing a flint (south quarter), and a final bowl containing fresh water (west quarter).

AT THE CENTER OF THE FOREST

In the mythos of the Rose and Thorn Path of Witchcraft, there appears what is known as the Hallow. This is envisioned as a place that separates material reality from nonmaterial reality. The Hallow is neither one of these in nature, nor is it something that arises from the merging of the two defined realities. In this sense, it's considered to be mystical and sacred.

One way to think of the Hallow is to imagine an hourglass that uses sand to measure the passage of time. One globe of the hourglass represents nonmaterial reality, and the other is material reality. In the center between the two globes is a corridor that allows sand to flow back and forth. The middle point is neither of the two globes; it's what separates them and gives them distinction. It's a space unto itself. By analogy, the corridor of the hourglass is the Hallow.

The concept of the Hallow arose from a sense that in the deep wooded places, there was a center point. Searches for it in the vast forest would prove an impossible find, and yet the core idea endured and appears in tales of Quests in which heroes seek a hidden magical kingdom, castle, mountain cave, or island on a misty lake or ocean. It's there but cannot be seen unless revealed through uncommon ways.

In legends associated with the Hallow, there's one tale in which it's guarded by Seven Sisters who are magical beings. These are symbolized by the constellation of the Pleiades, which signifies a celestial connection. In occult tradition, the stars of the Pleiades indicate the location of the gateway between life and death. This gate floats and thereby moves its position, much in the same way as the mythical floating islands do in occult tales. When the Pleiades are closest to the horizon on our planet (November Eve), the gateway opens for spirits of the dead to walk again in the mortal world. On May Eve, the Pleiades are farthest from the horizon, and the gateway opens above the earth for reincarnating spirits to descend into the Material Realm. According to legend, at these times the Hallow shimmers and can be seen as light in the distance (either amidst the trees or over a forest meadow). When the Hallow shines, the Old Ones emerge from oak and boulder and move about freely.

7

THE MYTHOS

It's common among inner mystery traditions to possess a set of myths and legends. The tales are, of course, fictional in the larger sense while at the same time reflecting two themes. The first is designed to convey the views, beliefs, and spiritual elements of the system. In doing so, they are often about the deeds of heroes, entities, deities, and spirits. They work together to preserve the lore and the heart or soul of the system using them. In this light, the stories incorporate the tenets of the system into various events and themes.

The second purpose of a mythos is to try to bring an understanding to complex concepts, most of which fall into the category of the mystical or occult. In this sense, the interactions of characters in a story are actually a depiction of how energies interplay, conflict, resolve, and so on. This facet of a mythos is its inner meanings—the Mystery Teachings.

On the surface, a mythos contains known elements of the system in which it appears. Even though a mythos has a setting, characters, and events, none of them are meant to indicate a historical account, even when they may present themselves as such. Therefore, it's important to understand that there's a *mythical history* within a Mystery Tradition system. Often this includes the mythical history of the system as well as its mythical founders. A side benefit of a mythos is that it supports a personal sense of self-identity for the tradition and its members and initiates.

The members of a tradition share not only a bond through knowing the inner tales, but they also together partake of the power that flows from the source of the stories in a mythos. The myths touch upon the deepest roots of the esoteric knowledge that have been cultivated and nurtured over countless centuries. These are the things that withstood the test of time; they are the time-honored and time-proven ways passed to us in a spiritual lineage of Witchcraft.

With this entire perspective kept in mind, let us now enter into the Mythos of the Old World Witchcraft.

NIGHT

In the beginning there was only Night, the endless blackness. Within her formlessness was nestled all that can ever be but isn't yet. Being alone, Night dreamt of companions, and upon awakening she birthed the stars, sun, and moon. From the shimmering light, she formed all the gods but kept to herself secret worlds that were later to be revealed. Because the gods were sad, having no world of their own, Night formed the earth for them. Upon the foundation of the earth, the gods built their towering cities above it.

There was, hidden in secret behind the moon, a black python that entered Night as she slept, and from this union was born three daughters. When the moon shows no light, the Three Daughters of Night walk together upon the earth. There, beneath the moonless sky, appears the ancient one known as the Washer in the Night. For all who come to her, she rinses their minds, soaks them in ancestral blood, and scrubs their bones clean so that honor is restored to their lineage.

PYTHOS, THE GREAT SERPENT

There was, in the vast black time of the Beginning, the starry serpent known as Pythos. Not desiring to share the starry sky, he gathered the fallen stars together into one place. Pythos coiled around them and formed them into one company. Then he burrowed deep into the earth, being seen no more.

In the time of People, Pythos spoke to them through vaporous crevices and caverns in the earth. Through his mystical, vaporous breath, he enchanted them, and he granted them visions of the future through his star-eyes. Feeling alone inside the earth, Pythos blew his star-breath outward and filled the blackness with bits of starlight that reminded him of his faraway home in the night sky. This was the creation of all the jewels within the earth that came to be treasured by people.

When the humans began to dig into the earth and take away these jewels, Pythos called out to the Great Night Sky, seeking aid to recover his star-shining jewels of the deep earthly realm. From this call came forth the creation of dragons, winged serpents that could fly from the deep caverns to the places of humankind in the world above. The dragons retrieved the jewels and returned them to the realm of Pythos, hiding and protecting them in great caverns from all who yearn for the sparkling gems.

KAELIFERA

Kaelifera, she who is the great star-being, once observed humankind from her celestial abode. From above, she beheld the plight of humans struggling to survive, being less equipped than the other animals on the earth that were naturally better suited to endure the environment. This stirred her compassion and moved her to take action. From her place in the starry night, Kaelifera wished to bring enlightenment to the people below. She wished to brighten their minds and ease their burdens.

At this time, the star-beings were constrained by a barrier separating the celestial from the terrestrial, but Kaelifera struggled to free herself from the bonds that held the stars fast. In a sudden burst of intense power, she broke free, but the momentum was so great that it caused her to race uncontrollably toward the earth. The star hit the earth with such impact that she penetrated down into its very center. Smoke and dust filled the crevice and remained for nine nights.

As Kaelifera slept in the deepest slumber, Pythos the Great Serpent came to her and impregnated her. (*Impregnation by a serpent during sleep is a very old theme. Sleep is the time of dreams, and dreams belong to the Other Realm. The inclusion of serpent impregnation within a story is always a supernatural event. It's not a rape, but is meant to indicate a passive receptive state, as in a mystical trance.*) Three days later, Kaelifera awoke and gave birth to a red dragon, which she named Vepres (pronounced veh-press). In this way, star and earth, celestial nature and terrestrial nature, joined as one.

After nine nights, the light of day made the opening to the surface of the land (left behind by the star's impact) visible. When night came, Kaelifera made her way back out, resting along the way on seven ledges that jetted out in the cavern tunnel left by the fallen star. After leaving the seventh ledge, Kaelifera was free and stood beneath an open sky.

Kaelifera returned to the night sky, but because of her love for her dragon child, she could not remain forever in the heavens. So she continues to descend to be with Vepres beneath the earth in the dragon's lair and then rises again to the sky as she wills. She can be seen as the morning and evening stars.

VEPRES, THE DRAGON

The ancient dragon known as Vepres was born in the depths of the earth. Its mother was Kaelifera, the star that entered into the earth. Its father was Pythos, the Great Serpent.

When Kaelifera descended from the starry realm, her passage into the earth split in half a great ancient tree that stood at the spot.

Vepres grew for three nights in the womb of Kaelifera and then was born within a cavern deep in the earth. This cavern was the most ancient of all places, and it bore the memories of all that lived and died in the world above. A fire burned in the cavern and gave a soft light that dimly cast its glow. Within the cavern, an opening formed into an inner realm, becoming a gateway, a sacred grotto. A deep pool of water formed in front of the grotto and can be reached only through the Well of the Moon.

In the cavern's light, Kaelifera looked upon the red body of the dragon. Along the dragon's spine showed a row of spikes in the fashion of rose thorns. The head of the dragon sported two large thorny horns, its teeth shaped like rose thorns, and red scales covered its body in the manner of armored rose petals. The wings of the dragon resembled shingled layers of rose leaves.

When the time came, Vepres rose upward from the passage that burrowed into the center of the earth. The dragon soon emerged from the tunnel into the world of light. It came to rest for a moment at the base of the ancient tree that was split by the descending star. There, Vepres breathed star-fire upon the rift in the tree and joined it back together. But the star-fire transformed the tree, turning it white, after which it shimmered with mystical light. Once transformed in this way, the white tree became a mystical gateway between the world of mortal-kind and the Otherworld of spirit-kind.

With the appearance of Vepres in the mortal world, a guardian-ship was established through which all entrances and exits between the worlds became protected.

THE WHITE TREE

The most ancient of all trees stood on the center of the earth, and it watched the Ages pass. Old legends told that the race of people was born from this tree. One eventful night, a great star raced down from the sky and split the tree in half as it passed into the earth below.

The tree groaned over its wound for seven nights and may have perished, had not something quite magical taken place. A red dragon emerged from the crevice left by the star and took notice of the tree in its cleft state. Understanding that this was the great Mother Tree of all, the dragon breathed a breath of star-fire onto it, which closed the rift and healed the tree. Such was the power of the star-fire that the tree glowed white from that day forward.

Like the stars themselves, the White Tree could now only be seen at night. Its starlight branches reached upward to the moon, for it was now of earth and sky. As the branches and roots of the tree grew and spread, its light shone into the Otherworld—the place of Faery. Soon the White Tree joined the worlds of mortal-kind and spirit-kind together. But its shimmer did not miss the attention of those in the Hidden Places.

From the sacred woods of the moon, the Seven Sisters descended to bless the White Tree so as to honor She of the White Round. The Faeries of the Lantra, who are bearers of the Star Lantern, passed virtue into the White Tree, which extended the Realm of the Faery to border in the center of the tree. In this way, the White Tree overlapped the mortal realm and the Faery Realm, and the Fey called it the White Tree of Faewyn. The Seven Sisters passed virtue into the tree as well and called it the White Tree of LuNeya—the realm of the moon.

The White Tree of Faewyn allowed for a passageway between the worlds, and the Faery used it to cross freely into the world of human-kind. It shimmered in their realm to indicate the magical portal, and from that day forward, meetings between people and Faery took place. To guard against discovery of this direct passage, the Faery created hollow mounds in the world of humankind, and these mounds existed at the tips of the roots of the White Tree. Inside the mounds, isolated areas of the Faery Realm were extended, and when mortals were allowed entry (as some were on occasion) the places looked like great dining halls. These rooms did not allow penetration by mortals into the Great Faery Realm itself, unless accompanied by a Faery traveler.

The White Tree was joined not only with the Realm of the Faery, for the Seven Sisters wielded the shimmer as well as did the Fey. In this way, others claimed it as the White Tree of LuNeya.

The starlight branches that touched the moon became bridges for the souls of the dead to journey to LuNeya (in which they took rest and prepared for rebirth). For the moon is the abode of the dead, and She of the White Round receives their light until she's full; then she rebirths these souls into the mortal realm. When all are reborn, the moon becomes dark and unseen, for the light of souls has passed once again from the heavens.

THE SEVEN SISTERS

In the Sacred Grove of LuNeya, there once lived a band of maidens who attended their Queen. This was long before the time when beings of light would come to dwell within bodies of clay. No one remembered birth, and no one knew of death. There was only LuNeya and its meadows, forest, and the sacred mountain.

When Night birthed the Clay-Born, death came into existence. Taking pity upon the spirits of the dead who wandered the earth, the Queen of LuNeya took them into her care. The Seven Sisters gathered them up at each crossroads, and brought them to LuNeya. Here their light was added to the realm, which shone brightly in the great blackness of Night Sky.

One evening when the Sisters journeyed to the earth, they encountered a large White Tree. Thinking it was a curious thing, they examined the tree by touching it with their hands. As they stood with the White Tree, its branches extended up into the sky until they embraced LuNeya. As the White Tree shimmered in the night, its light drew the spirits of the dead to where it stood. The Seven Sisters saw that they could easily escort the dead along the branches of the White Tree into the realm of LuNeya.

It was not long after finding the White Tree that the Seven Sisters beheld a far-off glow deep in the Great Forest. Wondering if this was another White Tree, the Sisters went to the place of light. Here they came upon a wondrous thing, for before them was a dazzling column of brilliant multicolored light. It separated all things, and it swirled in the center, guarding against one thing, touching another. Realizing that this could only come from divinity, the Seven Sisters called it the Hallow. In the Hallow, all things lose identity, and there's no conflict, disharmony, or order to things. There's only the way into all things.

When the Seven Sisters became the escorts of the dead, people spoke of them as the White Fey Women. The Queen of LuNeya, impressed at seeing that the Seven Sisters took up greater tasks, transformed them into stars to honor them. They left the forest of LuNeya and guarded the Hallow on earth against discovery, and they opened the Gates of Life and Death in the heavens. These gates appear on the Eve of May and the Eve of November.

THE LANTRA

There came a time when the barrier between the worlds of Faery and mortals opened in a mysterious way. At the unseen place between these worlds, a White Tree appeared not long after a great shining star rushed down upon the earth. The tree grew on the spot where the star disappeared deep into the earth; but this was no average tree.

The tree between the realms shimmered with starlight and was not solid in nature. The Faery Race learned that it could be penetrated and that it opened into another realm of existence. From that time forward, Faeries entered the mortal realm and had experiences with humankind. These encounters resulted in the tales told by people about the Faeries, but these experiences were always interpreted by humans through their limited awareness and understanding.

One group of Faeries came to be called the Lantra, the Keepers of the Star Lantern. This lantern contained a light that could not be extinguished, for it came from a star, and it illuminated even the darkest of places. This is called the Light-Bringing Star of the Nocturnal Mysteries, and it was given by Kaelifera, the Star Queen from the Great Night Sky. The Lantra were sworn to keep the Star

Lantern safe and to bear it against all who wished to block out light and leave only darkness.

In the Thorn Path of Witchcraft, Faeries are known as the People of the Blue Flame. The lore behind this tells that a rapid fanning or flickering blue fire showed from behind the Faeries when they appeared in the mortal realm. People mistook this phenomenon for wings, and so in legend, Faeries are often depicted as winged. Faeries require the blue flame in order to travel from their realm and back again.

THE REALM OF FAEWYN

Beyond the realm of the mortal world, past the gates of the rising and setting sun and moon, lies the land of Faery. It's called Faewyn, the White Realm of the Faery. Here, there's no natural death, and nothing is still or idle. The land of the Faeries, and all within it, gently flows from one point to another. A mortal in Faewyn cannot see this motion and believes that things appear and disappear in this realm. The eyes of mortals move too slowly and fix upon moments of time instead of what becomes of time. Mortals see where things were, not where they are, and in doing so they become subject to barriers that form as a result. These barriers are known by the terms *past, present,* and *future.*

Faewyn is a realm that resembles the lands and bodies of water known in the mortal world. It has day and night and seasons. The sun, moon, and stars are seen overhead, but they are reflections from the mortal realm. Light in the Faery World comes from the land within the realm itself, an energy that emanates from all things.

The proud cities of Finias, Falias, Gorias, and Murias were the glory of Faewyn until the ethereal armies of a jealous god drove the Faeries from them. The Faeries found refuge in the world of mortal-kind, where they awaited the time when they could retake their lost places. When the One God came into the world of humankind to displace the Many Gods, his armies left the land of Faewyn and took up battle with the Old Ones of the earth. It was then that the Faeries began to withdraw from the mortal realm, returning to their home in the shimmering realm of light.

THE REALM OF LUNEYA

In the endless black sea was an island city of the dead, which was known as Morphos. The city sat on the shore, where it was seen by all who approached it from the sea. Morphos was surrounded by woods and meadows in which grew poppies and mandrakes. In the center of the island stood a mountain with a cave in it, near its top. The cave opened into the Cavern of She of the Crossroads.

On the earth, at the sacred crossroads, stood the Great White Birch. For such did it appear to be in the mortal world. From the Hidden Realm, it was the White Tree that shimmered to call the dead. So it came to be called the White Tree of LuNeya, and around its branches the seven stars of the Seven Sisters (who escort the dead) glowed.

The souls of the dead travel in the branches of the White Tree, which are bridges crossing the endless black sea. When souls arrive, they are given rest and are prepared for another lifetime in the mortal world. They are purified in the Cavern of She of the Crossroads, and they drink from the springs of memory and forgetfulness.

When the time for rebirth arrives, souls travel back to the mortal world on the branches of the White Tree. In the land of the living, they descend from the Gate of Life and, guided by the Seven Sisters, the souls await the womb in which a new body will be fashioned.

THE HALLOW

When Night brought forth the creation of the earth, the realms of the manifest and the non-manifest could not touch. For if they did, both would disappear into each other and be gone for all time. To prevent this from happening, the Source of All Things placed an agreement between them, and this came to be known as the Hallow. It's neither a form or formless; it's what exists in-between them.

The Hallow stands in the center of the Great Forest of the Ancestors, the primordial world that's hidden by time to all who believe in time. The voices, thoughts, and prayers of humans and Faeries pass into the Hallow but are not heard or answered by it. They move through it and into other realms, for the Hallow is the corridor with endless portals to all worlds. Answers come from the Hallow but are not of the Hallow.

It's said that when the Hallow shines, something passes from one world into the next. The Seer perceives light in the center of the Great Forest, and for one brief shining moment, the secret place of the Hallow is known.

To draw the attention of the Hallow is to enter into the center of the light of one's own soul. In doing so, there's no self to be found; there's only the in-between space where the soul and that which created it look upon each other. It's a hallowed place.

8

THE OLD RITES

The rites practiced by our ancestors were designed around their needs and their understanding of the world (as well as the Otherworld). In Western Culture, the oldest written tales of Witches and their rites appear in fictional stories about them. These tales reflect the period beliefs regarding Witchcraft and therefore provide us with an understanding of the nonfictional elements woven into the ancient tales. What we find behind the scenes is the depiction of Witchcraft as very primal, carrying connections to beliefs that the stars, moon, mountains, and rivers possessed power. These could be called upon, summoned to the Witches' magical desires. The Witch was depicted as being in partnership with these forces and even with certain goddesses such as Hecate, Diana, and Proserpina. One very old element was the invoking of the powers of Night itself.

The old rites of Witchcraft place the Witch at the center of all things. She or he controls or directs the forces that are not understood by non-Witches. The Witch has inner or mystical knowledge of life and death, calls upon the dead as allies, and is a Seer into the Otherworld. This is one of the reasons why the Witch was both feared and respected in the pre-Christian world.

DRAWING THE MOON DOWN

This ritual is the root idea of connecting with the moon. The round moon is traced on the ground beneath it with the feminine stang, and the circle serves as a focal point for ritual and magic. The idea is that when you stand in the Round, you stand in the "Moon on earth." The moon then becomes a portal that links you through time to all Witches who ever called to the moon in their rites. As you stand in the Round, beneath your feet is the organic memory of the earth. Through this, you are connected to all the rites ever practiced by Witches whose feet have also known Shadow. In the Round, the timeless is drawn from above and from below.

To begin drawing the moon down, take the feminine stang and trace a circle on the ground (begin facing east and move in a clockwise direction). Next, take the stang to the east quarter. Hold it up with your left hand (the top end up toward the moon). Walk clockwise along the inside of the circle's edge with the palm of your right hand gliding over the circle's edge, and say:

> "That which in the sky is seen,
> Above, below, and in-between,
> Light and earth, the two I wed,
> They are one where now I tread."

Once this is completed, go to the south quarter and move clockwise as you sprinkle ivy leaves mixed with thorns all along the edge of the circle. As you do this, say:

> "Ivy, bind the earth and moon, lest they stray,
> Blessed thorns, keep spirits of ill intent at bay."

Complete setting the Round by lighting a fire in the direct center of the circle. Indoors, you can use a metal pot to hold the fire. The circle is ready for magic or ritual work.

THE DARK MOON RITE

The purpose of this ritual is to connect with the primal forces in the moonless night. It also serves to place the Witch in the hands of the Washer in the Night who dissolves away personal facades and the bondage to imposed social conformity. In this, the Witch returns to the untamed nature that lives deep in the heart of all Witches. Bear in mind that this rite isn't a turning away from civilized ways but is instead a rebooting of the original state of being. It's not a state of being to remain in, only to refresh oneself in and then continue on with material existence.

The rite of the Dark Moon is performed each of the three nights when the moon is black. Each night, one of the Three Daughters of Night is evoked. This requires the use of three colored candles, one black, one red, and one white. The black candle represents Potia, the red is Arrea, and the white is Timia. Each has a glyph for evocation, and this is placed in front of their respective candles.

In addition to the candles, you will need a bowl of fresh water and an area to bathe in. You will also need a lancet or a needle for pricking your finger, and a metal pot that can withstand burning paper inside it. Do not use pewter because it can melt.

After sunset on the first night of the dark moon, prepare your ritual area. Set the three colored candles side by side a few inches apart. Place the seal of Potia in front of the black candle and light the candle, saying:

> "I call to Potia, the first Daughter of Night,
> Look now with favor upon this rite."

Remove all clothing, jewelry, and adornments of any kind, saying:

> "I remove my connection to all facades and coverings that I bear."

Now, say:

> "I stand now as I was born before others added to me."

Move to your bathing area, taking with you the bowl of fresh water. When you're ready, say these words and then pour a portion of the water over your head:

> "Washer in the Night, rinse away all that constrains me, limits me, diminishes me, and moves me to compromise. Wash me clean down to the center of my being."

Do this three times.

Next, while still being wet, speak the dark truths about yourself that you share with no one—shout them out. Speak without shame or regret, just simply utter the facts. Elaborate upon what you declare about yourself. None of us is perfect, and so there's something to air in this solitary moment in the dark of night. After this, thoroughly dry yourself with a towel.

On a piece of paper, draw a large circle and mark an X inside it. When finished, look at the image and say:

> "Here are my truths unseen like the moon in the three dark nights."

Fold the paper and set it aside for now.

Now, look into the flame on the black candle and make affirmations about what you feel are the strengths (the things you would openly share about yourself). Don't attach emotion to them; just state them as facts. When finished, pick up the folded paper and draw a large crescent moon shape on one side of it. Using a pair of metal tongs, light the paper on fire from the candle and burn it in your cauldron. Make sure the entire paper is turned into ash. Place the ash in a jar until it's needed on the night of the first crescent.

Extinguish the black candle, clean up the area, but leave the candles in place.

On the second night of the dark moon, prepare the setting as you did the first night (except for the bathing). Place the glyph of Arrea in front of the red candle. Light the candle and say:

"I call to Arrea, the second Daughter of Night,
Look now with favor upon this rite."

Pause for a moment, and then prick your finger with a needle, squeeze three drops of blood into a cup of water, and say:

"Washer in the Night, soak me in the living river of blood
that flows from generation to generation. Fill me from the
center of my being."

Light the black candle, set it next to the red candle, place both palms over the cup of water, and say:

"I reach deep into the Cavern of the Ancestors, and draw
from the ancient well. May the Cauldron of Memory
awaken within me, and may the ancestors speak from the
blood we share in common, for I am the living lineage
bearer of all who came before me."

Place your fingertips on the carotid artery on your neck and feel your pulse for a few moments. Sense that this is the drumming of your ancestors throughout time. After this, dip your fingers into the water three times and sense the presence of your ancestors. Complete the night's ritual by pouring the cup of water outside on the base of a tree. Extinguish both candles.

On the third night of the dark moon, prepare the setting as before. Place the glyph of Timia in front of the white candle. Light the candle, and say:

> "I call to Timia, the third Daughter of Night,
> Look now with favor upon this rite."

On your work area, set the container of ashes from the first night. Light the black and red candles. Place the palms of your hands over the ashes, and say:

> "Washer in the Night, scrub clean the bone memory that binds generation to generation. Renew the center of my being."

Now, go to the north quarter, face south, and then stand so that your arms and legs form an *X* configuration. Speak the affirmation:

> "I am Pharmakeute!
> Roots beneath, hear me,
> Shadow below, know me.
> Branches above, connect me,
> For in-between I stand
> As a Thorn-Blooded Witch of the Ways."

Next, look at the three burning candles and say:

> "To the Three Daughters of Night, I give thanks for the blessings of liberation, the illumination in the places of darkness."

Now, take up the bowl of water and carry it, counterclockwise, from the east in a full circle. This represents the dissolving process of the Dark Moon rite. Then, facing east, turn counterclockwise to face the west. Carry the bowl over the west quarter, while saying:

> "I give thanks to the Washer in the Night for cleansing and restoring to me the untamed spirit of the Witch."

Set the bowl of water at the west, and then return to the north quarter and face south. Take up the X posture again and say:

> "By the rite of the Dark Moon, I reclaim the Witches' power,
> Washed and renewed am I, in the sacred moonless hour.
> She of the Crossroads, Lady of the Black Sacred Night,
> I honor you in darkness, and beneath the moon shining
> bright."

Sit outdoors and spend a few moments looking into the starry night sky. When you feel it's time, pour out the water on the ground. Next, take the ashes, say the following words, and then blow them to the west:

> "I bid the Three Daughters of Night to take my words of
> unspoken truths, both chaff and grain, shift through them,
> keep what is worth keeping, and with a breath of kindness
> carry the rest away upon the wind."

You can give offerings at this time, sing songs, or whatever makes you feel in celebration. Extinguish all the candles and clean up the area.

THE FULL MOON RITE

The light of the moon has long been associated with a mystical and magical nature. Many ancient tales contain the message that moonlight transforms, and it bestows wondrous things upon those who bathe in its light. In this context, Witches gather beneath the moon to drink in its light and enter into the sacred.

For this ritual you will need the sacred stone, feminine stang, masculine stand, human skull figure, ivy leaves, and rose thorns. Begin the rite by drawing the circle (of the moon) on the ground with the feminine stang. Fill a bowl with fresh water (about two-thirds full) and then position it so that the moon is reflected on the water. Look at the moon's reflection. Then close your eyes, lift the bowl to your mouth, and drink some of the water. Next, carry the bowl to the east quarter and present it, saying:

"Moon on the water, light in the night,
   Awaken the ways of the Witches' rite."

Turn around, clockwise, and walk to the west quarter where you will set the bowl on the ground. Take up the stang and go to the east quarter. Then, once again, trace over the circle on the ground (moving in a clockwise direction) as you hold the stang up with the top end toward the moon.

Next, beginning again at the east, walk along the inside of the circle's edge with the palm of your right hand gliding over the circle's edge, your left hand raised to the moon, and say:

"That which in the sky is seen,
   Above, below, and in-between,
   Light and earth, the two I wed,
   They are one where now I tread."

Once this is completed, go to the south quarter and move clockwise as you sprinkle ivy leaves mixed with thorns all along the edge of the circle. As you do this, say:

"Ivy, bind the earth and moon, lest they stray,
   Blessed thorns, keep spirits of ill intent at bay."

Complete setting the Round by lighting a fire in the direct center of the circle. Indoors, you can use a metal pot to hold the fire. The circle is ready for you to continue the Full Moon rite.

Begin at the east quarter and hold a lighted candle in your right hand. Then speak the opening words:

"On this night of the full moon,
   I come beneath the sacred light.
   And stand in the presence of She of the White Round,
   And He of the Deep Wooded Places."

Place a white candle at each quarter point of the Round, lighting each one in turn, and saying:

"To the Round, I add my light."

Return to the east quarter and blow your candle out (symbolically sending the flame back to the eastern candle).

Go to the center fire and say:

"Hear me Old Ones,
 For I come this night
 To make offerings to you
 As a sign of my devotion."

Place the offerings of your choice at the east quarter (fruit or grain are traditional offerings). Once offerings are placed, you can sing, drum, or chant to accompany this period of making the offering. After this, return to the center fire.

Fill a small bowl with water and then hold up the sacred stone, saying:

"Look now upon the sacred stone of the devotee,
 Keeper of the memories and spirit of the old ways.
 Through it I am never parted,
 Through it, nothing is ever forgotten."

Next, place the sacred stone inside the bowl of water, carry it to the west quarter, and set the bowl in place. Facing west, call to the ancients:

"I call out into the hidden mists to the ancestors, to all who have trod the Old Path of Witchcraft before me. Gather now in this time and place."

Pause for a moment to allow the ancestors to connect, and then retrieve the stone and take it to the east quarter where you will dry it with a cloth. Then return to the center fire.

Safely pass the stone three times over the fire (from left to right). Next, take the stone to the west quarter and say:

"I am a Thorn-Blooded Witch of the Ways,
I join with the spirit of the sacred stone here,
I join all of my kin."

Quickly pass the stone over the west candle flame, and say:

"Together are we."

Carry the stone to the east quarter and place it on the circle's edge. Leave it there until the end of the rite.

From the east quarter, walk around the entire circle and say:

"I am in the sacred Round,
I have carried the sacred stone of the Ways,
And I am one with all my kin who walk the sacred Round this night."

Next, take the masculine stang and carry the skull to the west quarter. With the stang in the right hand and the skull resting on the palm of the left hand, say:

"I call to She of the Crossroads,
Who aids all enchantments
And befriends the Witch,
Be now of favor and hold open the western gates
So I may have union this night
With those of the Ways who dwell on the other side."

Insert the branch end of the stang into the western wall of the Round, move it from left to right (as though parting a curtain) and then lay it on the ground (partly breeching the circle's edge).

Put the skull down and then place a lighted red candle on top of its head (if desired you can also make the blood offering by pricking your finger and letting three drops of blood flow into a bowl of water. The dead taste the blood and remember life, and then become animated within the Round).

Prepare the Feast of the Round, set a plate and cup for the dead, and then eat and drink in celebration. Speak whatever words you feel called to voice. Offer remembrances of those now crossed over, and don't forget to tell them you still love them.

[spend some time being receptive to communication]

At a chosen time, announce the end of the feast, and then say:

"The time has come now for you spirits to return to your realm.
I call upon She of the Crossroads to gather them now.
All return now to the Other Land, all return now.
In the name of She of the Crossroads,
All return now."

(Use the stang to usher the dead into the West quarter, and repeat three times:

"All return now.")

Blow out the red candle on the skull, and then pull the stang back into the circle. Next, point the branch end to the west and swing it from right to left (as in closing a curtain). To finalize, lower the stang to meet the ground inside the circle (place it to your left).

Cup the skull with your hands over its eyes and say:

"The gates to the Land of the Dead are closed,
And all have returned.
I have honored the departed, the ancestors,
And my Witch kin with celebration and feasting.
None are forgotten, nothing is ever forgotten."

Hold the skull up with both hands on the temple area of its head and say:

"As it was in the time of the beginning, so is it now, so shall it be!"

Lay the skull to rest at the west quarter. Next, prepare for veneration of deities. Set the masculine stang upright at the east quarter. Place offerings in front of the stangs. Then raise the stang up, placing it in front of your view of the moon, and say:

> "I behold She of the White Round and He of the Deep
> Wooded Places.
> Look with favor this night upon one who holds you in
> [her/his] heart.
> Accept these offerings that I have placed before you,
> And please bestow upon me your blessings that bring pros-
> perity, health, well-being, and enrichment to my life. Always
> will I keep to your Ways."

(Spend a few moments gazing upon the union of branch and moon.)

To honor the presence of the deities, start at the east quarter where you extend your left hand out, palm down. Slowly walk around the circle's inner edge, saying:

> "The moon above, the moon below,
> The sacred Round, the light to sow.
> The Greenwood herbs cast to encircle, for 'tis the old way,
> Hold the black sacred night and the bright blessed day."

(Complete the full circle from the east and then circle back again.) Standing at the east quarter, say:

> "I give thanks to the Old Ones, all spirits in the Hidden
> Places, and to the Elder Gods of my ancestors. I venerate
> She of the White Round and He of the Deep Wooded
> Places."

Prepare the sacred meal of union. Set the cake and wine together for blessing, hold the wand over them, and say:

"Blessings upon this meal, which is as my own body. For without this, I would perish from this world. Blessings upon the grain, which as seed went into the earth where deep secrets hide. And there did dance with the elements, and spring forth as flowered plant, concealing secrets strange. When you were in the ear of grain, spirits of the field came to cast their light upon you and aid you in your growth. Thus through you I shall be touched by that same Race, and the mysteries hidden within you, I shall obtain even unto the last of these grains.

Blessings upon this wine. When you were fruit on the vine, you drew to yourself the water that fell from the sky and flowed beneath the earth. There you gained the knowledge of the essence of the Overworld and Underworld, and contained this as you grew between the worlds. Thus through you I shall be touched by those mysteries, those hidden within you, and I shall obtain them even unto the last drop of this liquid brew."

Using the wand, trace an *X* over the wine, saying:

"By virtue of this sacred tool,
Be this wine the vital essence
Of the divine."

Do the same gesture over the cake, saying:

"By virtue of this sacred tool,
Be these cakes the vital substance
Of the divine."

Hold both palms over the meal and say:

"Through these cakes and by this wine, may She of the White Round and He of the Deep Wooded Places bless me, and give me inner strength and vision. May I come to know that within me, which is of the eternal gods. Blessed be all who partake of the divine."

Eat a portion of the cake, drink a portion of the wine, and save the rest for libations after the ritual is completed.

Finish the rite by looking up into the night sky. Remain receptive to any communication that may come to you. Afterward you can perform any spells or oracle work. When you are ready to leave, perform the following:

Go to the center fire and address the Old Ones:

"Old Ones, in good will, I bid you farewell,
The branches call you home,
The night sky reaches to embrace you,
And so we part until the White Round unites us once again."

Beginning at the east quarter and moving counterclockwise, extinguish all the quarter candles. Then return to the fire, face north, and say:

"The sacred Round is lifted. I stand again in the realm of mortal-kind."

This ends the ritual.

RITE OF THE WHISPERING DEAD

Perform this simple rite when wishing to contact or honor the dead. The rite requires a skull figure, a set of crossbones figures, one red votive candle, a glass of red wine, and a small bowl of grains or fruit. Another item you can use is a bark peeling from the white birch tree (*Betula papyrifera*) upon which you can write brief messages to send to the dead.

Begin by placing the skull figure in the center of your work area. Cross the two "bones" in front of it. Next, set the wine and bowl (with contents) between you and the crossbones. On top of the skull, place the red candle.

Face both palms over the crossbones and say:

> "In the name of She of the Crossroads, I call for the portal between the living and the dead to open before me."

Reach over and separate the crossbones and line them side by side (about a foot apart) so that they form an open path to the skull. Then light the candle on the skull, saying:

> "Here shines the light of the dead. I welcome you at this place in-between."

Move the wine and offerings into the space between the crossbones, and place them just a few inches in front of the skull. Once in place, say the following:

> "Accept now these offerings. Taste and remember life, and in the memory of life remember who you were, and in remembering this, give voice so that we may commune."

Sit quietly and remain receptive to communication. Don't try to force or rush things. However, in this setting, you can ask questions or say anything you wish. Listen for the dead to speak within you. If using birch peelings, you can now write messages to leave for the dead. Place them on the edge of the circle there in the west.

When you're ready to conclude, simply reverse the steps you first took. In order, you will remove offerings, blow out the candle, cross the bones back over each other, and then say:

> "I give thanks for the presence of those who came before me. In the name of She of the Crossroads, I call the portal between the living and the dead to close and be secure."

The rite is ended. Remove all items and bury the food and wine outside in the earth.

THE DEWY RITE OF THE MOON

This is a simple rite for imbuing herbs with the mystical essence of the moon. This enhances spell casting through the ways of the Greenwood magic. All plants that are used for spell casting should be joined with the fluid connection to the moon. To begin, collect some dew in the early morning hours. Dew is heaviest in the morning following the night of the Full Moon (although weather conditions can affect this).

Collecting dew isn't easy and can be time consuming. One method is to use a thin paper napkin and dab it across the surface of leaves. Once the napkin is sufficiently soaked, squeeze out as much of the water as possible into a bottle. You may need more than one paper napkin, and avoid getting any bits of it in the bottle. If that happens, fish them out.

To begin the rite, go to where you will find dew on the leaves of trees, bushes, or plants. Take a white candle with you as well as a bottle to hold the collected dew (and the napkin). You will also need your mortar and pestle. Place the items on the ground together (or upon a cloth). Then light the candle and say:

> "I carry forth the light of the moon into the day, and burn this torch in the name of She of the White Round."

Pick up the napkin and stand overlooking a dewy leaf. Say the following words and then start collecting the dew:

> "Lady of the Moon, in days of old you were called the Dewy One. Your liquid essence is now upon the Green Realm, and your dew is the sparkling emerald jewels of the night. I gather them up in your name."

When you are ready to squeeze the dew into the bottle, speak these words just before doing so:

> "Lady of the Moon, Lady of the Green Magic, I ask that you pass your virtue into this collected dew, and imbue it with your mystical nature."

Depending upon the amount of dew available and the size of your bottle, you may need to use the napkin several times. Each time it's used, you will repeat the words of enchantment spoken in each step.

When the bottle contains enough dew, place it in the mortar. Then pick up the pestle and hold it, tip down, over the bottle, and say:

> "I join you to the Greenwood magic through this mortar and pestle. Be moon-blessed and star-blessed so that through you the liquid light from above becomes the water of life below."

End by tapping the pestle against the inside rim of the mortar three times and then saying:

> "In the name of the Lady of the Moon and Stars, so be it."

Wrap the bottle in a cloth and store it away from direct sunlight. Extinguish the candle and then remove all the items as you depart the area.

The liquid is used to anoint the pestle for empowering herbs with a magical charge. When a fresh supply of herbs is ready for spell casting, place the needed portion in the mortar. Then moisten the tip of the pestle with the dew from the bottle and lower it so that it touches the herbs. Pause for a moment and then move the pestle over the herbs in a clockwise manner, saying:

> "I wake the spirit within, by the sacred dew of She of the White Round. And I stir the Lady of the Green to quicken the Greenwood magic."

The herbs are now aligned and charged for casting a spell in general. You will still need to incorporate your intention and work with the pertinent spell to manifest it.

THE WELL OF THE MOON

The purpose of this rite is to vitalize your psychic nature and your attunement to the Otherworld in general. This rite requires a black bowl (mini-cauldrons are useful) that you will fill two-thirds full with fresh water. You will also need a white rose. During the rite, wear a special piece of jewelry that you will only wear when working with psychic energy (and never just for personal adornment).

On the night of the full moon, begin by placing the white rose in the container of water. Then place both hands over it and say:

> "In the name of She of the White Round, be this the Well of the Moon."

With the fingers of your left hand (moving clockwise) trace the rim of the container three times while saying:

> "Here beneath the moon's full light,
> With the sacred key of the rose of white,
> I open the way through the Well of the Moon,
> To a realm that calls with the mysteries' tune."

Now, lean your head back so that you can see the moon above you. Pause for a moment, and then simultaneously lean forward quickly and drop your head forward so that it comes down over the Well of the Moon (this should feel like you dove from the moon down into the well).

Sense that you are deep in the water of the well, and then swim seven strokes forward under the water (in the manner of a frog—the breaststroke). At the seventh stroke, swim upward. Sense that you come up into a pool of water inside a cavern. Leave the pool and walk onto the shore. In front of you is a grotto opening. Walk over to it and stop just short of the entrance.

Sense that a female figure dressed in white emerges from the grotto. She hands you an orb of moonstone that shines like the moon. This is the stone of the Seer. You receive the stone and sit on the ground with the opening to the grotto in front of you. The woman stands and looks upon you kindly.

Sit quietly and receptively. The orb passes its light into your forehead. You feel a soft shimmering feeling there as it empowers your psychic center. Remain sensing this for a few moments. When you feel that the time has come, hand the orb back to the woman. She receives it, emanates a feeling of warmth toward you, and then turns to walk away into the grotto.

It's time to return. Walk back over to the pool and slip down into the depths of the water. Swim back as you came, seven strokes to reach the well. On the seventh stroke, physically sense that you forcefully surge upward and emerge from the well water. Confirm this with the sensation of holding the container and looking down at the water.

Conclude by standing and looking up at the moon. Touch your piece of jewelry and then say:

> "I bear the white light that shines from the secret realm beyond the Well of the Moon."

This concludes the rite. Remove all the items from the area and pour out the water onto the earth. Afterward, when performing psychic work, touch the piece of jewelry and say:

> "While I wear this [name it] may the light of Seer-stone shine within and without."

RITE OF THE TRIDENT

The purpose of this rite is to connect you with your magical character and nature. The rite will also move you into claiming your mastery. The only item required for this rite is a bottle of master oil, which is easily obtained through most Witch shops. If necessary, you can substitute this with your favorite personal scent (cologne or perfume).

Begin the rite by setting three candles in front of you—one black, one red, and one white. Light the black candle and say:

> "Potia, I renew my dedication to the Ways. Look upon me with favor."

Light the red candle and say:

> "Arrea, my blood runs true in the Ways. Look upon me with favor."

Light the white candle and say:

> "Timia, I preserve and continue the Ways."

Next, using the fingers of your right hand, trace a trident over the three candles while saying:

> "Above, below, and in-between."

Then face both palms toward the candles and say:

> "I am Pharmakeute, the Thorn-Blooded Witch. I have prevailed through challenge, proven worthy of crossing the thresholds, and I bear the passion that allures the moon and stars."

Now, beginning with the east quarter, trace a trident in the air at each of the four directions, saying:

> (East) "Upon the wind my words convey!"

> (South) "Into the flames my words transform!"

> (West) "Into the waters my words flow to embody!"

> (North) "Into the earth my words manifest!"

Next, looking at the three candles, quickly and safely *pinch* each flame on the candles (not putting them out) in a snatching manner, and say:

> (Black candle) "I wield the blackthorn!"

> (Red candle) "I wield the rose thorn!"

> (White candle) "I wield the white thorn!"

Now, anoint yourself with master oil as follows: left wrist, right wrist, heart area. Then raise your left hand up with the middle finger, index finger, and thumb pointing upward (other fingers folded) and say:

"I wield the Witches' Trident and bear its mysteries!"

Conclude by gently pressing your thumbnail against your lips and carefully placing the tip of the index finger under the left eye, and the middle finger under the right eye. In this posture, spend a few moments owning your experience, dedication, and love of the Ways. This posture of the Witches' Trident can also be used to direct and focus your mind when casting spells or working with energy.

9

THE MODERN
SOLITARY RITES

In contemporary times, the model of the Wheel of the Year is popular among many Pagans, Wiccans, and Witches. These, of course, are the eight seasonal festival periods of the year, which are often referred to as the Sabbats. In the Rose and Thorn Path of Witchery, when such modern rites are used, they're designed to present the Mythos of the Divine within Nature as the seasons flow, one into the other. In this light, the Mythos follows a mated Goddess and God (the personifications of the celestial and terrestrial emanations of divine presence and action) throughout the year. It's a complete and cohesive story that also presents esoteric concepts in the telling of it.

One of the differences in the modern rites, when compared with systems such as Wicca, is the use of the terms Sacerdotessa (pronounced Sah-chure-doh-tess-ah) and Sacerdote (Sah-chure-doh-tay). These words refer to the role of keeping things sacred within a tradition, ritual, or circle of the arts. In Old World Witchcraft, any formal group of Witches practicing together is called a Grove, which is a term in keeping with the idea of the connection to the Greenwood Realm. In essence, this is like the idea of a Coven in other traditions of Witchcraft.

Unlike many forms of modern Witchcraft and Wicca, we do not use the Elements or Elemental Spirits/Rulers as they're envisioned in contemporary practice. Instead, we use the concept of the elements as the essence or nature of the creative energies known as earth, air, fire, water, and air. Through this concept, we reach back to a time before humans added anthropomorphic views to the inner mechanism of Nature. Therefore, in Old World Witchcraft, we call each element by the title Asthesia (pronounced ah-thay-zah) and therefore we call upon the Asthesia of earth, air, fire, and water. Each is the raw energy of a specific elemental nature and quality (as opposed to a sentient spirit or entity).

Another difference between the modern festival rites of the Rose and Thorn Path and those of Wicca and modern Paganism is the use of names or titles. We intentionally use different ones so that people don't bring with them their preconceived ideas and views. If we were to use the title Samhain, for example, there's a predisposition to think about the rite as Celtic rooted and to expect certain popular practices and themes to be present. Our titles do not automatically evoke a cultural expectation or mind-set, which allows them to be experienced in their own right. The rites of the Rose and Thorn Path are a non-cultural expression of seasonal shifts and the mythology that personifies them.

Our Wheel of the Year begins on November Eve and is called Gadrian, which is an old word meaning "to gather" or "gather in." In our mythos, Gadrian is the Otherworld time when the feminine and masculine polarities of divinity are personified as the Lady of Shadow and the Lord of Shadow. It's the season of the enveloping blackness of procreation from which all things issue forth into the world of light. There in the shadowy realm, the Goddess and God mate, and she becomes pregnant with the seed of light passed into her by the God.

The next festival is called the Winter Tide and is performed on the day of the Winter Solstice. In the mythos, the Goddess gives birth to the new Sun God, who is called the Child of Promise (the promise being another year of light, life, and prosperity). At this time, we use the titles Lady of the Womb and Lord of Rebirth.

On the Eve of February, we celebrate with the rite known as Herthfyre, which is named after the sustaining hearth fires during Winter. In this season, we use the titles Lady of Fire and Lord of Ice. The land is frozen and requires the seductive fire of life to liberate it. This is the mythos of the slumbering seed and the stirring passion of the Womb of Nature.

The Wheel of the Year then turns to the Spring Tide, which is celebrated on the Vernal Equinox. At this time, we use the titles Lady of the Lake and Lord of the Reeds. In this season, the indwelling forces of Nature quicken the life force, and in turn the seeds beneath the earth issue forth into new plants for the season. The snow is melting, and fluids return to the life force.

Next comes the season known as Meadwey, a name derived from an old term for the meadow. It's celebrated on May Eve. At this time, the Goddess is called the Lady of the Green and the God is called the Lord of the Green. In the mythos, this is the time of courtship and intimacy between the couple. Fertility emanates into all things.

With the arrival of the Summer Solstice, we celebrate the Summer Tide. In this season, we use the titles Lady of the Flowers and Lord of the Woods. This is the pivotal point where the waning forces of the year lead Nature into the season of decline here in the midst of fullness. It's the magical in-between place.

Next is the seasonal shift to Harfest, a name derived from an old word meaning "harvest." It's celebrated on August Eve. At this time, we use the titles Lady of the Fields and Lord of the Barley. It is the time of the anticipation of the full harvest season.

Completing the annual cycle, we arrive at the festival of the Autumn Tide, which is celebrated on the Autumnal Equinox. At this time, we use the titles Lady of the Harvest and Lord of the Sheaf. Here the seed bearer willingly surrenders his life and falls into the earth. It is the act of renewal for the seasons to come again in the new year.

SETTING AND EMPOWERING THE ALTAR

The altar is essentially the center and focal point that connects to the Hallow, and through this to spirits and deities. It occupies the direct center point of the ritual or magical circle. In this way, it symbolizes the Hallow, which stands in the center where material reality and nonmaterial reality meet.

The altar establishes a portal or gateway between the worlds and the inner planes. This is represented by fire, either in the form of a lighted candle or an oil lamp. The flame occupies the center spot. Fire, as a primal divine image, establishes the presence of divinity within the circle.

> 1 goddess candle (red)
>
> 1 god candle (black)
>
> 1 center oil lamp/fire bowl (alternative: blue candle)
>
> 1 skull-topping candle (seasonal deity color)
>
> Rose pentacle (symbol of the Mystery Rose, five-pointed star)
>
> Human skull figure
>
> Wand
>
> Sacred Stone
>
> Cauldron
>
> Bell
>
> Incense

Orient the altar to face the east quarter. Lay a black cloth to cover the altar. This represents the procreative blackness from which all things issue forth. Place seasonal décor as desired.

Set the lamp/fire bowl directly on the center of the altar. This represents the sacred in-between place called the Hallow. In front of this, set the rose pentacle.

Set two altar candles (representing the feminine and masculine polarities of the divine) at the back of the altar, separated, each placed at the far end of the altar. The color of the Goddess candle is red, and the God candle is black. Next to the altar candles, an image of the Goddess and God can be placed if desired.

Between the candles/images of the deities, place a representation of a human skull. This symbolizes the knowledge and wisdom of our spiritual lineage that's preserved and passed on through the Old Ways. A black candle is set on the head of the skull and is lighted for all rituals performed from the Autumn Equinox until the Spring Equinox. A red candle is used from the Spring Equinox until the Autumn Equinox. Black symbolizes the ancestral knowledge retained within shadow and its connection to the realm of the Otherworld. Red symbolizes the ancestral knowledge that flows from the Otherworld to the world of mortals. It's the living river of blood that flows through the generations of Witches.

During the course of the year, the color of the skull's candle changes to match either that of the Goddess or God candle. Black represents the secret Shadow Realm, the deep dark forest, and the mystical journey that leads to the Otherworld. The God is the escort of the dead who aids in transition. Red represents the life's blood, the inner pulse that sustains and empowers. Regarding its connection to the Goddess, this current runs through the earth beneath the soil (for she's the giver of life). Red symbolizes the vehicle of life and renewal, which is reflected in the menstrual blood cycle. In the context of the skull figure, red symbolizes the ancient river of blood flowing into the world of the living. It flows from the ancestral memory retained in shadow, which is the source of its wellspring.

In front of the skull on the altar, place a small cauldron (or bowl), which contains the sacred stone. The cauldron represents the Well of the Moon, which in this context is the womb of the Goddess. Through the Goddess, all things are birthed from the Otherworld and are returned to her again. Therefore, the cauldron leads to and from the ancestral knowledge and opens into the Realm of Shadow. Because of this, it contains the magical essence of transformation.

Light the incense and place it where desired—this serves to carry the words of the rite into the ether.

Ring the altar bell thrice. Light the center flame on the altar and say:

> "I illuminate the in-between place, and draw now upon the sacred Hallow."

Ring the altar bell thrice. Light the goddess candle and say:

> "I evoke the presence of She of the White Round,
> And call upon her presence in this time and space."

Ring the altar bell thrice. Light the god candle and say:

> "I evoke the presence of He of the Deep Wooded Places,
> And call upon his presence in this time and space."

Hold up the rose pentacle and say:

> "By my right of crossing through the Thorn Gate,
> And by the powers risen in me from the Gathered Thorns,
> I call this portal open, and I maintain this sacred altar."

Ring the bell three times.

Tap the pestle inside the mortar three times and declare the altar set.

SETTING THE ROUND (THE RITUAL CIRCLE)

  1 broom

  4 quarter bowls for the Asthesia

  3 feathers (for Asthesia bowl)

  1 red candle (for Asthesia bowl)

  Purified water (for Asthesia bowl)

  Freshly dug soil (for Asthesia bowl)

4 white candles for quarter marking

2 Deity candles

Hallow candle

Mortar and pestle

Bell

Anointing oil

Stang

To begin setting the Round, take your broom and ritually sweep the physical area where the circle will be marked out. Then use the end of the feminine stang to etch the perimeter of the circle in a clockwise manner. Once completed, use the broom to sweep the air above the perimeter. Begin in the east and work around the circle clockwise until you return to the east.

Place the physical altar directly centered inside the circle. Arrange and activate it as prescribed by rite.

Place the four bowls of the Asthesia at each cardinal point of the Round: east, south, west, north. In the eastern bowl, place three feathers. The southern bowl contains a lighted red candle. The western bowl is filled with clean water, and the northern bowl contains newly dug earth. While placing each bowl, call upon its Asthesia to empower it and establish the elemental force:

To call the Asthesia of air, fan the feathers against the ground and then above your head, as you speak the words of calling:

"I call the Asthesia of air.
Come and send forth my intention."

To call the Asthesia of fire, light a red candle and place your left palm over the flame (close enough to feel the heat but not so close as to burn your skin). Then speak the words of calling:

"I call the Asthesia of fire.
Come and cause the change of my intention."

To call the Asthesia of water, cup some of the water in your hands and then allow it to trickle back into the bowl. Repeat this as you speak the words of calling:

> "I call the Asthesia of water.
> Come and bring movement to flow my intention."

To call the Asthesia of earth, pour some soil into your hands and compress it between your palms. Then speak the words of calling:

> "I call the Asthesia of earth.
> Come and bring solid form to my intention."

After placing the bowls and calling the Asthesia, return to the altar. Hold the palms of both hands safely above the center flame and call to the Hallow:

> "I call to the Hallow
> The center of purity
> The enduring unchangeable.
> I call to the Hallow,
> Suspend disbelief and belief
> So that all things are as they be.
> I call to the Hallow
> To bring me equilibrium,
> Balance and harmony."

Place both palms facing the candle on the left and call to She of the White Round:

> "I call to She of the White Round who commands the Night
> When secret mysteries are performed,
> I summon you.
> She of the White Round, bearer of souls in her care,
> Keeper of the cycle of life and death,
> From your cauldron do all things issue forth
> And return again.

I call to She of the White Round.
Look kindly now upon my intention
And manifest my desire."

Face both palms toward the candle on the right and call to He of the Deep Wooded Places:

"I call to He of the Deep Wooded Places,
Catcher of day and night,
Usher of Life and Death.
He of the Deep Wooded Places
Knows all that's seen in light and veiled in shadow.
You who provides sanctuary and safety in the Hidden Places,
I call to you.
He of the Deep Wooded Places,
Look kindly now upon my intention
And manifest my desire."

Finish by lighting the candle on top of the skull and then calling to She of the Crossroads:

"I call to She of the Crossroads,
Gatekeeper, Path Opener,
She of the Triple names.
Blessed trine,
Shine your light to reveal division.
Shed your light to reveal the ways.
I call to She of the Crossroads who commands silence
When secret mysteries are performed,
I summon you.
Night, faithful keeper of my secrets amid the stars, I call
to you.
She of the Crossroads knows all my designs
And aids the incantations and the craft of the Witches, I
summon you."

Now, take your wand in the left hand and pass it three times through the center flame on the altar. As you do so, speak these words:

"I draw from the Hallow."

Then pass the wand three times through the flame on the skull while saying:

"I call to memory within Shadow."

Next, hold the wand over the left altar candle and say:

"From She of the White Round,
I pass virtue into the circle."

Hold the wand over the right altar candle and say:

"From He of the Deep Wooded Places,
I pass virtue into the circle."

Go immediately to the eastern perimeter and switch the wand to your right hand. Point it down at the circle's edge, raise your left hand up into the air, and then walk along the edge from the east and back again. As you walk the Round, say these words:

"As above, so it's below.
Round is formed from head to toe.
Enclosing all, an Orb of light,
I set the Round and seal the site."

Take your pouch containing the mixture of crushed rue, vervain, St. John's Wort, rose petals, and ivy, and pour this into the mortar, and then sprinkle the blend along the perimeter of the circle. Begin at the east and return. As you move along the circle's edge, repeat the incantation:

"As above, so it's below.
Round is formed from head to toe.

Enclosing all, an Orb of light,
I set the Round and seal the site."

Tread the entire circle from east and back again while you slowly and rhythmically tap the pestle inside the mortar, saying these words of binding:

"Thu-ee tom tu-larr."

Beginning in the east and returning, tread the circle perimeter holding the rose pentacle outward toward the wall of the Round and say:

"I call upon She of the Thorn-Blooded Rose,
And bid you place your protection to encircle the Round,
And set your sharp thorns against any who would enter this place with ill intent."

All that remains now is to return to the altar and make the ritual knoll. To do so, ring a bell three times and then firmly tap the altar three times with the base of the wand. End by declaring:

"The Round is set."

DISSOLVING THE ROUND

The Asthesia are released by deactivating the forces at each quarter bowl. Beginning at the east and moving counterclockwise, place a cloth over each bowl (extinguishing the candle at the south before placing the cloth). As each cloth is laid, speak the words of release:

For air: "I release the Aesthesia of air to carry off its attachment to the Round."

For earth: "I release the Aesthesia of earth to crumble its attachment to the Round."

For water: "I release the Aesthesia of water to recede from its attachment to the Round."

For fire: "I release the Aesthesia of fire to cease its attachment to the Round."

At the altar, address the Old Ones:

"Old Ones, in good will, I bid you farewell,
    The branches call you home,
    The night sky reaches to embrace you,
    And so we part until the White Round unites us once again."

Now, extinguish both the left and right altar candles, saying:

"Hail and farewell!"

Address the Hallow:

"In good will I release the draw upon the Hallow.
    In withdrawing, all things here return to their former state.
    I stand once again in the world of mortal-kind,
    And the Hallow abides where all worlds meet."

Extinguish the center flame on the altar.

"I stand again in the realm of mortal-kind!"

Make this final announcement:

"The Round is lifted and released,
    The night revels are now deceased,
    Depart in peace without a sound
    Till we meet again in the sacred Round!"

GADRIAN (RITE OF NOVEMBER EVE)

Through this rite of Gadrian, you join with the forces of Nature that have retreated into Shadow. Here, their former state is dissolved into the Cauldron of Renewal, the formlessness from which all forms emerge. Gadrian is the presence and expression of these principles within the material world. When you touch this in the outer experience of Nature at this season, you connect it with the inner divine spark of consciousness within you. In doing so, you join material reality with spiritual perception, which brings about the wholeness of understanding.

To begin the ritual, set your altar with an appropriate theme décor such as a skull and crossbones, fall leaves, or other pertinent symbolism. The focal point of the altar is the mortar and pestle. The following items should be on hand:

> 2 candles to represent the presence of the Divine Feminine and Masculine
>
> Incense of your choosing (something earthy is good)
>
> Some fallen leaves (birch is best if possible)
>
> Mortar and pestle set
>
> 1 bone
>
> 1 skull figure
>
> 1 red candle to go with the skull
>
> 1 pot of soil (filled two-thirds full)
>
> Seeds of your choice as personal offerings to the deities
>
> Mystery cords (black, red, and white)

To begin the ritual after setting the Round, first state your intention/purpose:

> "At this season of Gadrian, the time of the gathering,
> I embrace the presence of formlessness drawing to itself all
> that had formed in the preceding seasons.

Through this time of season, the Great Mysteries are absorbed into Shadow where they return to the bone memory of the land.
The barrier thins and the formless spirits now walk freely among the living."

Place pictures of deceased friends and loved ones on or near the altar. Place a candle on top of the skull, and set food and drink for the dead. Put the leaves around the base of the skull. Then say:

"I place this sacred meal of remembrance for those who have departed from the realm of the living."

You can speak the names of your loved ones, speak to them, or simply send your love. This is the personal time to do so.

Light the altar candles representing the Divine Feminine and Divine Masculine forces. Then place the mystery cord in front of the feminine candle and say:

"The season now passes to the Watch of the Goddess. I call to the Lady of Shadow, the dissolver and transformer of weary forms, and I call to the Lord of Shadow, the shaper of formless things in the vapor of shadow beneath the earth."

Hold up the mortar and say:

"I evoke and invoke the Death Taker.
I honor the Divine Womb into which all life returns,
And from which all life issues forth again."

Hold the pestle pointing downward and say:

"I evoke and invoke the Serpent Slumberer,
the waning messenger that lays to stillness the life that withdraws into the Divine Womb of new envisioned regeneration."

Tap the bone with the pestle three times, and then push the bone (lengthwise) down into the soil within the pot and say:

> "The God who was formerly slain, moves now in the liquid blackness within the Realm of Shadow."

Into the pot, drop the seeds one by one, and say:

> "These are seeds of form fallen into the cauldron of the formless. These are the elements of my own nature that await dissolution and transformation so that I escape the finite patterns of the past and prepare for the rebirth of my soul's light. Herein is the end of what was manifest, and what follows now is the immersion into the black pool of the moon well, wherein I am light at home in the darkness. From the Well of the Moon, I will rise up as the envisioned soul that can only be reshaped through that which first gave it life."

With the mortar placed on the altar, hold the pestle above it (pointing downward) and say:

> "I join with the cycle of the seed slumbering in Shadow
> I reach downward into blackness,
> and dissolve into the Cauldron of Transformation that sits within the organic memory of the earth.
> I give way to the unmanifest, and I dissolve away as the finite, so that I rise up from Shadow as the brightness of a new and greater star."

Hold both hands palm down over the mortar and say:

> "Here is the vessel of Shadow's brew. I release my state of being and slide into the womb of dissolution from which I came and to which I return. My immersion advances me toward manifestation anew."

Pause and remain still and quiet for a few moments—envision a moonless night sky.

Next, take the pestle and move it counterclockwise in the mortar, saying:

> "The guardian serpent swallows the seed, becomes the seed, and forms as seed again. I am that seed, the star seed, and I await rebirth in the season to come."

Now it's time to give offerings to the Old Gods. For this rite, the time-honored offerings are seeds. Other offerings can be given as well, such as earthy incense smoke, coins pressed into the soil, and the pouring of dark wine into the soil.

When giving offerings, say these words:

> "I give these offerings, and with heartfelt reverence, to the Lady of the Shadow who gathers forms from the mortal realm and reenvisions them into what they can become. Through you, all life is loses the finite and gains the whole. With love, I freely give these offerings to honor you, and I ask for your blessings of transformation and generation.
>
> I give these offerings, and with heartfelt reverence, to the Lord of the Shadow who moves unseen in the blackness of procreation. Through you, there's assurance of becoming once again. With love, I freely give these offerings to honor you, and I ask for your blessings of becoming, emerging, and attaining.
>
> As it was in the time of the beginning, so is it now, so shall it be."

Set the offerings in an open place outside. Next to the offerings, pour out the contents of the mortar.

Hold the pestle over the offerings and the soil, and say:

> "May these offerings be pleasing to the Old Gods, and be well received. May the seeds of desired transformation and emergence manifest in my life by the Lady of Shadow,

and may the Lord of the Shadow initiate my becoming in the star vision of light. And into the earth, woods, and fields may the life-giving blessings of the Old Gods breathe transformation and emergence."

Conclude the rite by giving thanks. You can play some music, sing, dance, or read a poem or favorite passage to in some personal way celebrate the theme of Gadrian as a closing to this seasonal rite. (As a meditative concept, for example, stir some sugar into some water and watch it dissolve and disappear. Then freeze the water, take it out, feel and taste it in its new form. Reflect on the idea of transformation from one form of expression to the next.)

End the ritual by releasing the Round.

WINTER TIDE (YULE)

Through this rite of the Winter Tide of Yule, you join with the forces of Nature that now rise up from the depths of Shadow and emerge into the living realm of mortal-kind. Here, what was previously dissolved back into its basic elements now takes form once again. Its essence, the ever-living light of the soul, is the presence and expression of these principles within the material world. When you touch this in the outer experience of Nature at this season, you connect it with the inner divine spark of consciousness within you. In doing so, you join material reality with spiritual perception, which brings about the wholeness of understanding.

To begin the ritual, set your altar with an appropriate theme décor such as an evergreen wreath and other pertinent symbolism of the season. The focal point of the altar is the mortar and pestle. The following items should be on hand:

2 candles to represent the presence of the Divine Feminine and Masculine

Incense of your choosing (something evergreen)

1 small figure to represent the sun god (The Child of Promise)

1 small basket for the sun god figure (or he can be placed inside the wreath)

1 small candle to represent the newborn light (gold is best)

Mortar and pestle set

Personal offerings of your choice to the deities

Mystery cords (black, red, and white)

To begin the ritual after setting the Round, state your intention/ purpose:

> "At this season of the Winter Tide of Yule, the time of the rebirth of never-ending light,

> I embrace the emergence of formation from formless Shadow, the child of light to call forth the sleeping seeds of regeneration that issue forth new life.

> Through this time of season, the Great Mysteries glisten upon the star seed of light.

> The light is born anew from within and without."

Place the sun god candle in front of the wreath. Then say:

> "I place this awakened light, the rays of hope, my soul's rebirth in which the promise of spiritual evolution shines forth. I break company with the season of decline and claim my place in the gift of waxing life."

Light the altar candles representing the Divine Feminine and Divine Masculine forces. Then place the mystery cord in front of the masculine candle and say:

> "The season now passes to the Watch of the God. I call to the Lady of the Womb, the Gateway and Deliverer of form

from formlessness, and I call to the Lord of Rebirth, the formation of light risen from the blackness—renewer and sustainer."

Hold up the mortar and say:

"I evoke and invoke the Life Giver.
I honor the Divine Womb, from which all life returns,
And from which all life issues forth again."

Hold the pestle pointing downward and say:

"I evoke and invoke the Serpent Awakener,
The waxing messenger whose shining rays of light dispel illusion,
And reveal the world anew once again.
The constrained view now gives way to the unlimited vision."

Set the pestle standing upright inside the mortar and say:

"The God who submerged into the liquid blackness within the Realm of Shadow is now risen, and stands once again in the world of mortal-kind. I rise and return with him, and my light is brightened through his rays."

Hold both hands palm down over the mortar and pestle, and say:

"Here is the vessel of the Divine Light reborn. I release my former state that slumbered in Shadow, and I unite with the new life of the new light that will grow strong and bring forth vitality, renewal, and abundance."

Remove the pestle, and then symbolically birth the Child of Promise from the mortar. Then place him on the wreath, which represents the undying cycle of life.

Take the pestle and move it clockwise over the wreath, saying:

"The Child of Promise is born, the light and life of the World is returned. The star seed assures renewal, and I am within the seed of light, and I am born to the new light. The year now turns to wax strong again, and with it I inherit the promise. I am the star seed, and I am born anew, and I wax full and strong with the growing light begun now in this season."

Now it's time to give offerings to the Old Gods. For this rite, the time-honored offerings are evergreen branches, wreaths, and other related symbols of enduring life. Other offerings can be given as well, such as woodsy incense smoke, pinecones, and the pouring of white wine into the soil.

When giving offerings, say these words:

"I give these offerings, and with heartfelt reverence, to the Lady of the Womb who births forms into the mortal realm, and bestows upon them the noble quest to grow in light. Through you, all life is awakened and returned, and the part rises and flows across the surface of the whole. With love, I freely give these offerings to honor you, and I ask for your blessings of growth, enlightenment, and empowerment.

I give these offerings, and with heartfelt reverence, to the Lord of Rebirth who moves into the world of mortal-kind and with the glowing seed of light that opens into the blossom of the sun. Through you, there's assurance of purpose and presence once again. With love, I freely give these offerings to honor you, and I ask for your blessings of emerging, growing, and reigning.

As it was in the time of the beginning, so is it now, so shall it be."

Set the offerings in an open place outside. Hold the pestle over the offerings and the soil, and say:

"May these offerings be pleasing to the Old Gods, and be well received. May the rekindled flame of light's return manifest in my life by the Lady of the Womb, and may the Lord of Rebirth fill me and carry me aloft in his light that will rule in the year to come. And into the earth, woods, and fields may the life-giving blessings of the Old Gods breathe vitality and new growth."

Conclude the rite by giving thanks. You can play some music, sing, dance, or read a poem or favorite passage to in some personal way celebrate the theme of Yule as a closing to this seasonal rite.

Reflect on the idea of the return of light in the time of seeming decline. Think on how the endless cycle of unvanquished life is connected to the sun and how light is carried in the vessel of the sun, which ever declines and ever grows back to full strength. See your life, and the light of your soul, as reflected in the seasons of the sun.

End the ritual by releasing the Round.

HERTHFYRE (FEBRUARY EVE)

Through this rite of Herthfyre, you prepare to join with the forces of Nature that await initiation, awakening, renewal, and vitalization. Herthfyre is the presence and the expression of these principles within the material world. When you touch this in the outer experience of Nature at this season, you connect it with the inner divine spark of consciousness within you. In doing so, you join material reality with spiritual perception, which brings about the wholeness of understanding.

To begin the ritual, set your altar with an appropriate theme décor such as a bare branch, dried leaves, a cup of snow or ice cubes, or other pertinent symbolism. The focal point of the altar is the mortar and pestle. The following items should be on hand:

2 candles to represent the presence of the Divine Feminine and Masculine

Incense of your choosing (myrrh is a good choice)

Some grain to symbolize the sleeping seed in the earth below

1 red candle

Ice cubes and a plate to place them on

Mortar and pestle set

Personal offerings of your choice to the deities (coins and grain are traditional)

Mystery cords (black, red, and white)

To begin the ritual after setting the Round, state your intention/ purpose:

> "On this eve of Herthfyre,
> I embrace the presence of suspension and liberation.
> Through this time of seasons, the Great Mysteries reveal
> The fullness of potentiality and the quickening forces that liberate.
> All flows forward in the red river of blood that sustains our existence."

Pass a hand over the lighted altar candles that represent the Divine Feminine and Divine Masculine forces. Then place the mystery cord in front of the Feminine candle and say:

> "The season now passes to the Watch of the Goddess. I call to the Lady of Fire, the liberator of endless and abundant life, and I call to the Lord of Ice, the Keeper of the burning flame of life."

Hold up the mortar and say:

> "I evoke and invoke the Life Liberator.
> I honor the Divine Womb whose inner fire forges all life,
> And unto which all life returns."

Hold up the pestle and say:

> "I evoke and invoke the Horn Awakener,
> The risen stalk that's aroused by the seductive fire of
> promise,
> And from that union issues forth the passion that leads
> to life."

Into the mortar, place some grains and say:

> "These are symbols of all that's bound to the frozen land.
> Herein is the measure of what came in the season past,
> And returns again in the season to come."

With the mortar placed on the altar, hold the pestle above it
and say:

> "I join with the cycle of the Greenwood Realm,
> I reach downward into that which is frozen and suspended in
> my own being,
> And I awaken the seed of renewal,
> And I invoke vitality that's the liberator of all that slumbers.
> Awaken, arise, and unite me with the forces of the Herthfyre
> season."

Turn the mortar slightly sideways and insert the pestle, slowly
moving it in and out, and say:

> "Seed to sprout,
> Sprout to leaf,
> Leaf to bud,
> Bud to flower,
> Flower to fruit,
> Fruit to seed."

Repeat this three times.

Set the mortar down to rest. Hold both palms downward above the mortar, making the gesture of the Triangle of Manifestation, and say:

> "Here I connect with all that needs awakening, renewed vitality, and liberation. I put forth my energy to rekindle vitality, renewal, liberation, and all that enriches my life. I join myself to this cycle of Nature and strengthen its reflection in my own existence. I call forth for the liberation from suspension in my life. May the sleeping seeds within all rise to thrive in the season to come."

Set a plate with a lighted red candle in the center. Surround the candle with ice cubes. Watch the ice cubes melting as you affirm the things that need liberation within you and state what you seek to gain from this liberation.

Now it's time to give offerings to the Old Gods. For this rite, the time-honored offerings are grain. Other offerings can be given as well, such as sweet incense smoke, coins pressed into the soil, and the pouring of liquid chlorophyll (the green blood of plants) into the soil. When giving offerings, say these words:

> "I give these offerings, and with heartfelt reverence, to the Lady of Fire who warms the seed of the Greenwood Realm and provides renewal for all living things. Through you, all life is sustained. With love, I freely give these offerings to honor you, and I ask for your blessings of liberation, passion, and vitality.
>
> I give these offerings, and with heartfelt reverence, to the Lord of Ice who bears the suspended seed that ensures the cycle of life. Through you, there's assurance of life renewed. With love, I freely give these offerings to honor you, and I ask for your blessings of the will to rise, grow, be vital, and thrive.
>
> As it was in the time of the beginning, so is it now, so shall it be."

Set your offerings in an open place outside. Next to the offerings, pour out the contents of the mortar.

Hold the pestle over the offerings in the ground and say:

> "May these offerings be pleasing to the Old Gods and be well received. May the fruits of desired manifestation be freed into my life by the Lady of Fire, and may the Lord of Ice release in me all that's still and unawakened. And into the earth, woods, and fields may the life-giving blessings of the Old Gods breathe renewal, vitality, growth, and abundance."

Conclude the rite by giving thanks. You can play some music, sing, dance, or read a poem or favorite passage to in some personal way celebrate the force of Herthfyre as a closing to this seasonal rite.

End the ritual by releasing the Round.

SPRING TIDE (VERNAL EQUINOX)

Through this rite of Spring Tide, you prepare to join with the forces of Nature that bring about renewal and continuation. The Spring Tide is the presence and expression of their principle within the material world. When you touch this in the outer experience of Nature at this season, you connect it with the inner divine spark of consciousness within you. In doing so, you join material reality with spiritual perception, which brings about the wholeness of understanding.

To begin the ritual, set your altar with a Spring theme décor. The focal point of the altar is the mortar and pestle. The following items should be on hand:

2 candles to represent the presence of the Divine Feminine and Masculine

Incense of your choosing (something floral is good)

3 seeds of your choosing to represent your goals this year

1 cup of rich garden soil

1 handful of grain (such as spelt, barley, or even rice)

Mortar and pestle set

Liquid chlorophyll

Personal offerings of your choice to the deities (coins, fruit, grain, flowers, and so on)

First, state your intention/purpose:

"On this day of the Spring Tide,
I embrace the presence of renewal and continuation.
Through this Tide, the Great Mysteries initiate
the Mysteries of birth, life, death, and renewal."

Light the altar candles representing the Divine Feminine and Divine Masculine forces and say:

" I call to the Lady of the Lake, the liberator of bound life within the land,
And I call to the Lord of the Reeds, the liberated fertilizing force within the land."

Hold up the mortar and say:

"I evoke and invoke the Life Giver,
I honor the Divine Womb from which all life issues forth,
And unto which all life returns."

Hold up the pestle and say:

"I evoke and invoke the Horn Awakener,
The impregnating force that stirs to life all within the Divine Womb."

Halfway fill the mortar with fertile soil, and then drop three seeds upon the soil. Next, say:

"These are seeds of my desire, these the things that grow to harvest in my life."

Name the seeds after whatever it is that you want to manifest in your life.

With the mortar placed on the altar, hold the pestle above it and say:

> "I join with the cycle of the Green World,
> I reach downward into Shadow,
> And I draw up the organic memory of the earth.
> Awaken, arise, and unite me with the forces of the Spring Tide."

Using the pestle, gently tap the seeds into the soil (the motion is up and down with slow and deliberate movement). While tapping, say:

> "Seed to sprout,
> Sprout to leaf,
> Leaf to bud,
> Bud to flower,
> Flower to fruit,
> Fruit to seed."

Repeat this three times.

Hold both palms downward above the mortar, making the gesture of the Triangle of Manifestation, and say:

> "Here are the seeds of my desire, and I send forth my will to manifest all that's good in life."

(You can name the thing you wish at this phase of the rite as well.)

Now it's time to give offerings to the Old Gods. For this rite, the time-honored offerings are grain (particularly spelt grain). Other offerings can be given as well, such as sweet incense smoke, coins pressed into the soil, and the pouring of liquid chlorophyll (the green blood of plants) into the soil.

When giving offerings, say these words:

> "I give these offerings, and with heartfelt reverence, to the Lady of the Lake who quenches the thirst of all who live in this world. Through you, life flows. With love, I freely give

these offerings to honor you, and I ask for your blessings of renewal, growth, and vitality.

I give these offerings, and with heartfelt reverence, to the Lord of the Reeds who satisfies the hunger of all who live in this world. Through you, the body is sustained. With love, I freely give these offerings to honor you, and I ask for your blessings of renewal, growth, and vitality.

As it was in the time of the beginning, so is it now, so shall it be."

Set the offerings in an open place outside. Next to the offerings, pour out the soil from the mortar.

Hold the pestle over the offerings and the soil, and say:

"May these offerings be pleasing to the Old Gods and be well received. May the seeds of desire be watered by the Lady of the Lake, and may the Lord of the Reeds grow and raise my desires so that they manifest in full and rich harvest this year."

Conclude the rite by giving thanks. You can play some music, sing, dance, or read a poem or favorite passage to in some personal way celebrate the force of Spring as a closing to the Spring Rite.

MEADWEY (MAY EVE)

Through this rite of Meadwey, you prepare to join with the forces of Nature that bring about the fertilization and the impregnation within, which itself leads to regeneration. The Meadwey seasonal shift is the presence and expression of these principles within the material world. When you touch this in the outer experience of Nature at this season, you connect it with the inner divine spark of consciousness within you. In doing so, you join material reality with spiritual perception, which brings about the wholeness of understanding.

To begin the ritual, set your altar with an appropriate theme décor such as flowers and other pertinent symbolism. The focal point of the altar is the mortar and pestle. The following items should be on hand:

> 2 candles to represent the presence of the Divine Feminine and Masculine
>
> Incense of your choosing (something floral or sensual is good)
>
> A vase of flowers
>
> Mortar and pestle set
>
> The Green Blood (Liquid chlorophyll)
>
> Bowl of fresh water
>
> Personal offerings of your choice to the deities (coins, fruit, grain, flowers, and so on)
>
> Mystery cords (black, red, and white)

To begin the ritual after setting the Round, state your intention/ purpose:

> "At this time of Meadwey, I embrace the fertilizing forces and natures that call spirit to manifest in form. Through this time of season, the Great Mysteries of life take root in the flesh, drawing the Mysteries of birth, life, death, and renewal back into the world of mortal-kind."

Light the altar candles representing the Divine Feminine and Divine Masculine forces. Then place the mystery cord in front of the Feminine candle and say:

> "The season now passes to the Watch of the Goddess. I call to the Lady of the Green, the temptress of abundant life, and I call to the Lord of the Green, the Risen Stalk to bear ripened grain into the season to come."

Hold up the mortar and say:

"I evoke and invoke the Life Giver, Death Taker.
I honor the Divine Womb that receives the seeds of life,
And by which all life issues forth again."

Hold the pestle pointing downward and say:

"I evoke and invoke the Horn Awakener,
The waxing messenger that arouses the generator of life,
Flowing the life essence into the Divine Womb of
regeneration."

Pour out some of the liquid chlorophyll into the bowl of water.
Then point the tip of the pestle down toward the mortar and pause
for a moment.

Move the pestle over to the bowl of water, dip it into the water,
and then lower it into the mortar and say:

"The fluid of the Lord of the Green bathes now the womb of
the Lady of the Green,
The mystery of birth buds in the world of mortal-kind."

With the pestle held upright inside the mortar, say:

"I join with the cycle of the life budding in the womb of
Nature.
I reach downward into Shadow and stir the organic memory
of the earth.
Awaken, regenerate, thrive, and unite me with the forces of
the Meadwey Tide."

Hold both hands palm down over the mortar and say:

"Here is the living essence of the Mystery of the Gate of
Thorns through which all life enters into the realm of
mortal-kind. Formless embraces form, and they become
one in the darkness of the womb."

Pick up the mortar and drink a sip after saying:

"I receive the flow that brought me from the hidden blackness, and the forces that carry me through the Tides of
Nature. My ascent delivers me into the fullness of the season
of flesh as my spirit moves through the Wheel of the Year."

(You can affirm the things you wish to gain in the months ahead
that lead to the Harvest Season.)

Now, lower the pestle into the mortar and say:

"I join with Nature, like attracts like."

Begin a rhythmic tapping back and forth inside the mortar while
saying:

"Seed to sprout,
Sprout to leaf,
Leaf to bud,
Bud to flower,
Flower to fruit
Fruit to seed."

Repeat this three times.

Now it's time to give offerings to the Old Gods. For this rite, the
time-honored offerings are flowers. Other offerings can be given as
well, such as sweet incense smoke, coins pressed into the soil, and the
pouring of liquid chlorophyll (the green blood of plants) into the soil.

When giving offerings, say these words:

"I give these offerings, and with heartfelt reverence, to the
Lady of the Green who births the life of the Greenwood
Realm and regenerates the fullness for all living things.
Through you, all life is re-formed and returned. With love,
I freely give these offerings to honor you, and I ask for your
blessings of growth, vitality, fruitfulness, and abundance.

I give these offerings, and with heartfelt reverence, to the Lord of the Green who offers the life-giving essence that ensures the continuing cycle of life. Through you, there's assurance of life renewed. With love, I freely give these offerings to honor you, and I ask for your blessings of renewal, growth vitality, fruitfulness, and abundance.

As it was in the time of the beginning, so is it now, so shall it be."

Set the offerings in an open place outside. Next to the offerings, pour out the contents of the mortar.

Hold the pestle over the offerings and the soil, and say:

"May these offerings be pleasing to the Old Gods and be well received. May the union of the Lady of the Green and the Lord of the Green Sheaf place into my hands the growth of new form in the seasons to come. And into the earth, woods, and fields, may the life-giving blessings of the Old Gods breathe new life, new form, renewal, vitality, growth, and abundance."

Conclude the rite by giving thanks. You can play some music, sing, dance, or read a poem or favorite passage in some personal way celebrate the force of the Meadwey Tide as a closing to this seasonal rite.

End the ritual by releasing the Round.

SUMMER TIDE (SUMMER SOLSTICE)

Through this rite of the Summer Tide, you prepare to join with the forces of Nature that bring about the fullness of life and enrich all things. The Summer Tide shift is the presence and expression of these principles within the material world. When you touch this in the outer experience of Nature at this season, you connect it with the inner divine spark of consciousness within you. In doing so, you join material reality with spiritual perception, which brings about the wholeness of understanding.

To begin the ritual, set your altar with an appropriate theme décor such as flowers, fruit, and other pertinent symbolism. The focal point of the altar is the mortar and pestle. The following items should be on hand:

> 2 candles to represent the presence of the Divine Feminine and Masculine
>
> Incense of your choosing (something floral or fruity is good)
>
> Mortar and pestle set
>
> 1 apple
>
> Knife
>
> Personal offerings of your choice to the deities (coins, fruit, grain, flowers, and so on)
>
> Mystery cords (black, red, and white)

To begin the ritual after setting the Round, state your intention/ purpose:

> "At this time of the Summer Tide,
> I embrace the manifesting forces and natures that call spirit into the fullness of form.
> Through this time of season, the Great Mysteries of life fill the flesh,
> Drawing the Mysteries of birth, life, death, and renewal back into the world of mortal-kind."

Light the altar candles representing the Divine Feminine and Divine Masculine forces. Then place the mystery cord in front of the Feminine candle and say:

> "The season now passes to the Watch of the God. I call to the Lady of the Flowers, the mother of abundant life, and I call to the Lord of the Woods, the protector of life as the seasons move one into the next."

Hold up the mortar and say:

> "I evoke and invoke the Life Giver, Death Taker.
> I honor the Divine Womb that has delivered life into form,
> And by which all life issues forth again."

Hold the pestle pointing downward and say:

> "I evoke and invoke the Horn Awakener,
> The waxing messenger that empowers the life force within Nature,
> Bearing the seeds of everlasting for the awaiting Divine Womb of regeneration."

With the knife, slice the apple in half from the stem area down to the bottom, and then separate the apple (you should see where the seeds are lodged). Then say:

> "Here is the Sacred Mystery, the seed of life nestled in the fullness of Nature."

Lay the tip of the wand on the face of the sliced apple and say:

> "Here is the risen stalk of life and the Cauldron of Regeneration. Through this union may the days ahead be evergreen."

Place one half of the apple in the mortar. Then lower the pestle down to meet it and say:

> "I join with the cycle of the risen stalk and ripening flesh of Nature's bounty.

I reach downward into Shadow and call to the organic memory of the earth.
Awaken, foresee, prepare, and unite me with the forces of the Summer Tide."

Hold both hands palm down over the mortar and say:

"Here is the living embodiment of the Mystery of Life.
Here is the hidden seed in the ripening abundance of Nature's bounty."

Pick up the apple half, say the following words, and then kiss the area where the seeds are contained:

"I venerate the forms within Nature that carry within them the Great Mystery of birth, life, death, and rebirth. Here is the symbol of those Mysteries placed before me by the Old Ones so that I will always remember."

Take a few moments and give thanks for all that's good in your life and all that you see as potential in the future.

Now it's time to give offerings to the Old Gods. For this rite, the time-honored offerings are flowers. Other offerings can be given as well, such as spicy incense smoke, coins pressed into the soil, and the pouring of liquid chlorophyll (the green blood of plants) into the soil.

When giving offerings, say these words:

"I give these offerings, and with heartfelt reverence, to the Lady of the Flowers who brings forth fullness in the life of the Greenwood Realm and prepares all living things for the season to come. Through you, all life grows to strength and fullness. With love, I freely give these offerings to honor you, and I ask for your blessings of growth, vitality, fruitfulness, and abundance.

I give these offerings, and with heartfelt reverence, to the Lord of the Woods who protects what has grown from within the Greenwood Realm. Through you, there's the strength of endurance and fortitude. With love, I freely give these offerings to honor you, and I ask for your blessings of renewal, growth vitality, fruitfulness, and abundance.

As it was in the time of the beginning, so is it now, so shall it be."

Set the offerings in an open place outside. Next to the offerings, pour out the contents of the mortar.

Hold the pestle over the offerings and the soil and say:

"May these offerings be pleasing to the Old Gods, and be well received. May the wedding of the Lady of the Flowers and the Lord of the Woods place into my life the sustaining forces of Nature in this season and those to come. And into the earth, woods, and fields may the life-giving blessings of the Old Gods breathe new life, new form, renewal, vitality, growth, and abundance."

Conclude the rite by giving thanks. You can play some music, sing, dance, or read a poem or favorite passage to in some personal way celebrate the force of the Summer Tide as a closing to this seasonal rite.

End the ritual by releasing the Round.

HARFEST (SEPTEMBER EVE)

Through this rite of Harfest, you prepare to join with the forces of Nature that bring about abundance, maturity, and reward of effort. Harfest is the presence and expression of these principles within the material world. When you touch this in the outer experience of Nature at this season, you connect it with the divine spark of consciousness within you. In doing so, you join material reality with spiritual perception, which brings about the wholeness of understanding.

To begin the ritual, set your altar with an appropriate theme décor such as a cornucopia or other pertinent symbolism. The focal point of the altar is the mortar and pestle. The following items should be on hand:

> 2 candles to represent the presence of the Divine Feminine and Masculine
>
> Incense of your choosing (something fruity is good)
>
> Several types of fruit and some grain to symbolize abundance
>
> Mortar and pestle set
>
> Personal offerings of your choice to the deities (coins, fruit, grain, flowers, and so on)
>
> Mystery cords (black, red, and white)

To begin the ritual after setting the Round, state your intention/purpose:

> "On this eve of Harfest,
> I embrace the presence of ripeness and abundance.
> Through this time of seasons, the Great Mysteries reveal
> The fullness of Life, the sacred river of blood that sustains
> our existence."

Light the altar candles representing the Divine Feminine and Divine Masculine forces. Then place the mystery cord in front of the Feminine candle and say:

> "The season now passes to the Watch of the Goddess. I call
> to the Lady of the Fields, the Birther of abundant life, and I
> call to the Lord of the Barley, the Bearer of ripened Nature."

Hold up the mortar and say:

> "I evoke and invoke the Life Generator.
> I honor the Divine Womb from which all life

comes to fullness,
And unto which all life returns."

Hold up the pestle and say:

"I evoke and invoke the Horn Awakener,
The risen stalk that arouses the coupling of Birther and
Breeder, and from that union issues forth the ripe seed bearer."

Into the mortar, place a portion of fruits and grains, and say:

"These are symbols of all that's rich and abundant. Herein is
measure of return from effort."

With the mortar placed on the altar, hold the pestle above it
and say:

"I join with the cycle of the Greenwood Realm,
I reach downward into Shadow,
And I draw up the organic memory of the earth.
Awaken, arise, and unite me with the forces of the Harfest
season."

Run the tip of the pestle clockwise around the edge of the mortar
and say:

"Seed to sprout,
Sprout to leaf,
Leaf to bud,
Bud to flower,
Flower to fruit,
Fruit to seed."

Repeat this three times.

Hold both palms downward above the mortar, making the gesture of the Triangle of Manifestation, and say:

"Here I connect with all the effort I put forth to bring
about abundance, richness, and prosperity in my life. I join

myself to this cycle of Nature and strengthen its reflection in my own existence. I call forth for the manifestation in my life all that's my due and full measure."

(You can affirm the things you wish to come to fullness in your life now.)

Now it's time to give offerings to the Old Gods. For this rite, the time-honored offerings are ripe fruit and grain. Other offerings can be given as well, such as sweet incense smoke, coins pressed into the soil, and the pouring of liquid chlorophyll (the green blood of plants) into the soil.

When giving offerings, say these words:

"I give these offerings, and with heartfelt reverence, to the Lady of the Fields who nurtures the Greenwood Realm and provides the fullness for all living things. Through you, all life is sustained. With love, I freely give these offerings to honor you, and I ask for your blessings of growth, vitality, fruitfulness, and abundance.

I give these offerings, and with heartfelt reverence, to the Lord of the Barley who bears the seed that ensures the cycle of life. Through you, there's assurance of life renewed. With love, I freely give these offerings to honor you, and I ask for your blessings of renewal, growth vitality, fruitfulness, and abundance.

As it was in the time of the beginning, so is it now, so shall it be."

Set the offerings in an open place outside. Next to the offerings, pour out the contents of the mortar.

Hold the pestle over the offerings and the soil, and say:

"May these offerings be pleasing to the Old Gods and be well received. May the fruits of desired manifestation be gathered into my life by the Lady of the Fields, and may the Lord of the Barley ripen and present them before my hands. And into the earth, woods, and fields, may the life-giving blessings of the Old Gods breathe renewal, vitality, growth, and abundance."

Conclude the rite by giving thanks. You can play some music, sing, dance, or read a poem or favorite passage to in some personal way celebrate the force of Harfest as a closing to this seasonal rite.

End the ritual by releasing the Round.

AUTUMN TIDE (AUTUMNAL EQUINOX)

Through this rite of Autumn Tide, you prepare to join with the forces of Nature that bring about the completion of cycles and the gathering of fullness in preparation for decline, which itself leads to regeneration. The Autumn Tide is the presence and expression of these principles within the material world. When you touch this in the outer experience of Nature at this season, you connect it with the inner divine spark of consciousness within you. In doing so, you join material reality with spiritual perception, which brings about the wholeness of understanding.

To begin the ritual, set your altar with an appropriate theme décor such as a cornucopia or other pertinent symbolism. The focal point of the altar is the mortar & pestle. The following items should be on hand:

> 2 candles to represent the presence of the Divine Feminine and Masculine
>
> Incense of your choosing (something earthy is good)
>
> A sheaf of wheat or a corn cob, or anything of grain
>
> Mortar and pestle set
>
> Ritual blade

The Green Blood (Liquid chlorophyll)

Personal offerings of your choice to the deities (coins, fruit, grain, flowers, and so on)

Mystery cords (black, red, and white)

To begin the ritual after setting the Round, state your intention/ purpose:

> "At this time of the Autumn Tide,
> I embrace the presence of completion and the shedding of
> old for new.
> Through this time of season, the Great Mysteries come
> full circle,
> Rejoining the Mysteries of birth, life, death, and renewal."

Light the altar candles representing the Divine Feminine and Divine Masculine forces. Then place the mystery cord in front of the masculine candle and say:

> "The season now passes to the Watch of the God. I call to
> the Lady of the Harvest, the gatherer of abundant life, and
> I call to the Lord of the Sheaf, the Giver of the ripened
> grain who falls into shadow beneath the earth."

Hold up the mortar and say:

> "I evoke and invoke the Death Taker.
> I honor the Divine Womb into which all life returns,
> And from which all life issues forth again."

Hold the pestle pointing downward and say:

> "I evoke and invoke the Serpent Slumberer,
> The waning messenger that lays to stillness the life that
> withdraws into the Divine Womb of regeneration."

Take the ritual blade and ceremonially "cut down" the Seed Bearer, and say:

> "The Harvest Lord willingly dies so that his seed and life falls into the womb of the Goddess. The Slain God journeys now into the Realm of Shadow."

Into the mortar, drop the seeds of grain one by one and say:

> "These are seeds of return, these are the elements of my own nature that await transformation and regeneration. Herein is the gathering of one full cycle of growth returning back into itself."

With the mortar placed on the altar, hold the pestle above it (pointing downward) and say:

> "I join with the cycle of the Sleeping Seed
> I reach downward into Shadow,
> And nestle in the organic memory of the earth.
> Await, slumber, rest, and unite me with the forces of the Autumn Tide."

Hold both hands palm down over the mortar and say:

> "Here are the fallen seeds of my transformation and the regeneration to come. I fall back into the arms of the forces from which I came and those that carry me through the Tides of Nature. My descent advances me toward renewal."

(You can affirm the things you wish to transform and the renewal that you will to manifest in your life.)

Now, anoint the pestle with the liquid chlorophyll and then lower it into the mortar, saying:

> "The green blood of the Harvest Lord has been sacrificed, and his ripened grain falls back into the earth:

Seed to Shadow,
Shadow to memory,
Memory to past,
Past to seed,
Seed to Greenwood,
Greenwood to seed."

Now it's time to give offerings to the Old Gods. For this rite, the time-honored offerings are ripe grain. Other offerings can be given as well, such as earthy incense smoke, coins pressed into the soil, and the pouring of liquid chlorophyll (the green blood of plants) into the soil.

When giving offerings, say these words:

"I give these offerings, and with heartfelt reverence, to the Lady of the Harvest who gathers the life of the Greenwood Realm and regenerates the fullness for all living things. Through you, all life is refreshed and renewed. With love, I freely give these offerings to honor you, and I ask for your blessings of growth, vitality, fruitfulness, and abundance.

I give these offerings, and with heartfelt reverence, to the Lord of the Sheaf who sacrifices the ripened seed that ensures the continuing cycle of life. Through you, there's assurance of life renewed. With love, I freely give these offerings to honor you, and I ask for your blessings of renewal, growth, vitality, fruitfulness, and abundance.

As it was in the time of the beginning, so is it now, so shall it be."

Set the offerings in an open place outside. Next to the offerings, pour out the contents of the mortar.

Hold the pestle over the offerings and the soil and say:

"May these offerings be pleasing to the Old Gods and be well received. May the seeds of desired transformation and renewal manifest in my life by the Lady of the Harvest, and may the Lord of the Sheaf release the ripeness and present this to my hands in the seasons to come. And into the earth, woods, and fields, may the life-giving blessings of the Old Gods breathe transformation, renewal, vitality, growth, and abundance."

Conclude the rite by giving thanks. You can play some music, sing, dance, or read a poem or favorite passage to in some personal way celebrate the force of the Autumn Tide as a closing to this seasonal rite.

End the ritual by releasing the Round.

MAKING GROUP RITES

Each of the solitary rites can be embellished to make it suitable for a group of people to perform. This is simply a matter of dividing up various phases of the rite and assigning them to a number of people in attendance. You can also add other things that you feel will allow more participation by members of the group.

For setting the Round (casting circle) with multiple people, I suggest the following additions, but feel free to add more:

- Assign a member (or members) to place the elemental bowls at each quarter.

- Assign a person to evoke the Asthesia at each quarter using the vowel sound tonal calls:

  East/Air: Eeeee

  South/Fire: Iiiiii

  West/Water: Ooooo

  North/Earth: Aaaaa

- Assign two people to perform working with the candles and the calls at the altar.

- Appoint a person to physically cast the Round by treading the circle as prescribed in the rite.

- Have all members carry a lighted candle as they walk around the circle. Each one goes along the edge of the circle and pauses to touch his candle flame to the flame on each candle at the north, east, south, west. When doing so, each person says: *"To the Round I add my light."*

For the eight festival rites (Sabbats), I suggest the following embellishments:

- Assign one person to give the opening address of the ritual's purpose/intent.

- Appoint two people to the mortar and pestle set (female for mortar, male for pestle).

- Select two facilitators to direct the members, one by one, into participating in the alignments performed with the mortar and pestle set. Remember to look for needed changes in the text (*we* instead of *I*). The facilitators should be opposite sex to represent and speak the respective Goddess and God alignment wordings. If the participants are gay or lesbian, then naturally the couple will work with the feminine and masculine inner polarities.

- Incorporate opportunities in the ritual for singing, chanting, drumming, and dancing. This will bring a stronger festive nature to the rite.

- Have members come forward individually when it's time to place offerings.

- Examine the Mythos (Her Story, His Story) and create ways for individuals to perform ritual plays to enact the Mythos during the ritual.

The modernized Mythos from Old World Witchcraft tells the tale of a mated deity couple and their journey through the seasons of the year. It's a cohesive story in which we find the key points that reflect the divine within Nature. The following outlines these points:

- Goddess and God meet.

- They engage in courtship.

- The Goddess is impregnated.

- The Goddess gives birth to Nature's bounty.

- The God dies with the Harvest of that bounty.

- Goddess descends into the Underworld to reunite.

- Goddess and God join in union once again.

- Goddess is impregnated with the Seed of Light.

- Goddess births New Sun God, the Child of Promise.

In the Mythos, there are two stories running in tandem. They feature the Goddess and God, respectively. Let's examine each separately in order to reveal the inner teachings.

Her Story

The Goddess is the Whole (the Everything), and in this sense, she represents the Wheel of the Year as a concept. She's the entire year reflected at once in the Wheel. In the Mythos, the Goddess never dies; she can't because she's the whole of existence. We can only catch a glimpse of her nature at each of the eight festivals:

- Gadrian: The Goddess is seen as the potential Creator of all things. Gadrian marks the beginning of the year, the time of procreation. The year begins in blackness, and the Goddess is known as the Lady of Shadow. At this time, the Goddess is pregnant with the Seed of Light inside her womb.

- Winter Tide: The Goddess is viewed as the Womb of Creation. She's the vessel through which the Seed of Light is born from the blackness into the world of mortal-kind. Her baby is the newborn sun, the Child of Promise for the coming solar year. At this time, she's known as the Lady of the Womb.

- Herthfyre: The Goddess is envisioned as the Formless Divine Flame Liberator. At this season the land is frozen and the seeds beneath the soil are bound to Winter's grip. The Goddess is the flame that thaws the land and arouses the seed. Her crown of torches designates her reign, and the Wheel of the Year must then turn to release what is bound in this season. At this time, she's known as the Lady of Ice.

- Spring Tide: The Goddess is revealed as the Source of Life and Fertility Fluids. The snow and ice are melting into liquid. Lakes awaken, and reeds issue forth along their edges. The essence of life flows now within the white-covered earth. At this time, she's known as the Lady of the Lake.

- Meadwey: The Goddess is seen as the Emergence of Life in Nature. The Greenwood has emerged in response to her presence. Here, the courtship between her and the God takes place, and she's impregnated. At this season, the Goddess is called Lady of the Green.

- Summer Tide: The Goddess is viewed as the Abundant Vessel of Rebirth. She's pregnant with Nature's bounty, having been impregnated in the season of Meadwey. In the Summer season, the Goddess is known as Lady of the Flowers.

- Harfest: The Goddess is envisioned as the Mother/Nurturer of Abundant Life. The ripe bounty of Nature shows in its fullness. This marks the entry into the Harvest season. At this time, the Goddess is called Lady of the Fields.

- Autumn Tide: The Goddess is perceived of as the Cauldron/ Receiver of Ripened Seed. The time for harvesting Nature's bounty is fully upon us. At this time, the Goddess is called Lady of the Harvest.

His Story

The God is the part of the Whole, the finite elements, and in this sense, he represents the points in the Wheel of the Year as a structure. He follows a mortal life pattern—he is born, matures, and dies. His death is linked to the Greenwood and the harvest of its bounty. He's the seed-bearer who, with his death, falls into land. The God can only be glimpsed as whole through each individual aspect that rises with each distinct season.

- Gadrian: The God is the Potential Generator of Life. Here in the beginning of the solar year cycle, all begins in black-ness. At this time, the God is in the Hidden Realm and is known as the Lord of Shadow. In the mystical sense, he is within the Goddess and not truly distinct from her. In this way, the Goddess contains him, is pregnant with him.

- Winter Tide: The God is the Seed of Light Formed. In this season, he's born from the realm of blackness into the world of light. He arrives as the Child of Promise, the newborn Sun God. At the Winter Tide, he's called the Lord of the Rebirth. This is the dawning of his awareness of separation from the whole, for he is now finite.

- Herthfyre: The God is the Bound Seed and is bound to for-mation. His vitality is restrained, frozen in the hold of Win-ter over the land. This is the trial of his realization that he is truly separate from the Whole, and this revelation moves him to seek his own expression and nature.

- Spring Tide: The God is the Fertile Generator of Life. Here, he finds and embraces his role as the Part that renews the

Whole with vitality. The Whole flows through Nature in fluid form, and the Part rises to meet it.

- Meadwey: The God is the Fertile Initiator and Vitality of Life. He penetrates the Whole with the life essence of the Part. The Whole responds with regeneration of the forms that can manifest in the material world.

- Summer Tide: The God is the Provider and Protector of Abundance. He preserves all that has been made manifest through the reunion of the Whole and the Part. Like a great and powerful stag, the God is ever vigilant to ensure the survival of all that he keeps in his watch.

- Harfest: The God is the Seed Bearer of life to come in the next season. The ripened life is the fulfillment of the Part and all that it carried forth from the Whole. It is the fulfillment of the covenant between life and death, hunter and hunted, harvest and harvester.

- Autumn Tide: The god is the Fallen Seed of Renewal. The ripened life dies back into the Whole from where it came, and in this, both become refreshed and revitalized. The Part is gathered so that it can rejoin with the Whole. In this, it's absorbed and its life experience merges with the mind of the Whole. In this season of the Harvest, the God falls back in the Hidden Realm. His absence draws the awareness of the Goddess, who must take him back into herself to renew her wholeness.

THE PLANT SPIRIT
SEALS

The following are the customary images used to evoke or invoke the spirits of the Greenwood magic in the Rose and Thorn Path. You can draw them on parchment, paint them on disks, draw them in ashes, or etch them into candles.

B

SYMBOLS OF THE ROSE
AND THORN PATH

The following are the customary images used in ritual and in magic within the Rose and Thorn system. They can be painted, drawn on, or etched on any ritual or magical object. The symbols can also be placed on ritual tools. Use one or more to assign power or significance to a tool or item of ritual/magic.

Abundance Attract Bind Banish

Discord Endurance Enchant Forsee

Good Fortune Harmony Hex Health

Love Block Protection Separate

Seduce Repel Reverse Transform

Thorn-Blooded Rose

White Round

Crossroads Lady

3 Daughters of Night

He of the Deep Wooded Places

LuNeya

Faewyn

Hallow

Manifest

Summon

Counter Magic

Release

Life-Giver

Death-Taker

Receive

BIBLIOGRAPHY

Abernathy, Francis E. *Between the Cracks of History: Essays on Teaching and Illustrating Folklore*. Denton: University of North Texas Press, 1997.

Alexiou, Margaret. *The Ritual Lament in Greek Tradition*. Lanham: Rowman & Littlefield Publishers, Inc., 2002.

Bailey, Cyril. *Phases in the Religion of Ancient Rome*. Berkeley: University of California Press, 1932.

Briggs, K. M. *The Anatomy of Puck: An Examination of Fairy Beliefs Among Shakespeare's Contemporaries and Successors*. London: Routledge and Kegan Paul, 1959.

———. *Pale Hecate's Team: An Examination of the Beliefs on Witchcraft and Magic Among Shakespeare's Contemporaries and His Immediate Successors*. London: Routledge and Kegan Paul, 1962.

Burne, Charlotte Sophia. *The Handbook of Folklore: Traditional Beliefs, Practices, Customs, Stories, and Sayings*. London: Senate, 1995.

Campbell, Joseph. *The Masks of God: Primitive Mythology*. New York: Arcana, 1991.

Cousineau, Phil. *Once and Future Myths: The Power of Ancient Stories in Modern Times*. Berkeley: Conari Press, 2001.

Davidson, H. R. Ellis. *Myths and Symbols in Pagan Europe*. Syracuse: Syracuse University Press, 1988.

Dyer, T. F. Thiselton. *The Folk-Lore of Plants*. Middlesex: The Echo Library, 2007

Éliade, Mircéa. *The Myth of the Eternal Return*. Princeton: Princeton University Press, 2005.

———. *Myths, Dreams, and Mysteries*. New York: Harper & Row, 1975.

———. *Patterns in Comparative Religion*. New York: Sheed & Ward, 1958.

———. *Rites and Symbols of Initiation*. Putnam, CT: Spring Publications, Inc., 1994

———. *The Sacred and the Profane*. Orlando, FL: Harcourt Books, 1987.

Ellis, Bill. *Lucifer Ascending: The Occult in Folklore and Popular Culture*. Lexington: University Press of Kentucky, 2004.

Filotas, Bernadette. *Pagan Survivals, Superstitions and Popular Culture*. Toronto: Pontifical Institute of Mediaeval Studies, 2005.

Fletcher, Robert. *The Witches' Pharmacopœia*. Baltimore: The Friedenwald Co., Printers, 1896.

Folkard, Richard. *Plant Lore, Legends, and Lyrics: Embracing the Myths, Traditions, Superstitions, and Folk-Lore of the Plant Kingdom*. London: Sampson Low, Marston & Company, 1892.

Grenier, Albert. *The Roman Spirit in Religion, Thought, and Art*. New York: Alfred A. Knopf, 1926.

Klaniczay, Gabor, and Popcs, Eva (Editors). *Witchcraft Mythologies and Persecutions*. New York: Central European University Press, 2008.

Hazlitt, W. C. *Dictionary of Faiths & Folklore: Beliefs, Superstitions, and Popular Customs*. London: Bracken Books, 1995.

Jones, Alison. *Larousse Dictionary of World Folklore*. New York: Larousse Kingfisher Chambers Inc., 1995.

Klaniczay, Gábor and Éva Pócs (eds). *Witchcraft Mythologies and Persecutions*. New York: Central European University Press, 2008.

Knight, Gareth. *The Rose Cross and the Goddess*. New York: Destiny Books, 1985.

Lang, Andrew. *Myth, Ritual & Religion*, vol. 1. London: Senate, 1995.

———. *Myth, Ritual & Religion*, vol. 2. London: Senate, 1996.

Matthews, Caitlin and John Matthews. *Walkers Between the Worlds*. Rochester, VT: Inner Traditions, 2003.

Murray, Grace A. *Ancient Rites and Ceremonies*. London: Senate, 1996.

Philpot, J. H. *The Sacred Tree in Religion and Myth*. Mineola, NY: Dover Publications, 2004.

Porteous, Alexander. *The Forest in Folklore and Mythology*. Mineola, NY: Dover Publications, 2002.

Propp, V. *Morphology of the Folktale*. Austin, TX: University of Texas Press, 1968.

Sharp, William. *Where the Forest Murmurs*. Freeport, NY: Books for Libraries Press, 1970.

Simoons, Frederick J. *Plants of Life, Plants of Death*. Madison, WI: University of Wisconsin Press, 1998.

St. Leger-Gordon, Ruth E. *The Witchcraft and Folklore of Dartmoor*. New York: Bell Publishing Company, 1972.

Thiselton-Dyer, T. F. *The Folk-Lore of Plants*. Middlesex: The Echo Library, 2007.

Thompson, C. J. S. *The Mystic Mandrake*. London: Rider & Co., 1934.

Vickery, Roy. *Oxford Dictionary of Plant Lore*. Oxford: Oxford University Press, 1995.

Von Franz, Marie-Louise. *The Interpretation of Fairy Tales*. Boston: Shambala Publications, 1996.

Wind, Edgar. *Pagan Mysteries in the Renaissance*. New Haven: Yale University Press, 1958.

Worthen, Thomas D. *The Myth of Replacement: Stars, Gods, and Order in the Universe*. Tucson, AZ: University of Arizona Press, 1991.

Yearsley, Macleod. *The Folklore of Fairy-Tale*. London: Watts & Co., 1924.

Zemkalnis, Jeronimas (trans.). *Cultural Wellsprings of Folktales*. New York: Manyland Books, Inc., 1970.

ABOUT THE AUTHOR

Peter Paradise Michaels for
RavenWolfe Photography.

Raven Grimassi is a Neo-Pagan scholar and award-winning author of over seventeen books on Witchcraft, Wicca, Magick and Neo-Paganism, including Old World Witchcraft and Italian Witchcraft. He is the co-directing Elder of the Ash, Birch and Willow tradition of Witchcraft, and is co-founder and co-director of the Fellowship of the Pentacle, a modern Mystery School tradition. He lives in Springfield, MA. Visit him online *at www.houseofgrimassi.com*

TO OUR READERS

Weiser Books, an imprint of Red Wheel/Weiser, publishes books across the entire spectrum of occult, esoteric, speculative, and New Age subjects. Our mission is to publish quality books that will make a difference in people's lives without advocating any one particular path or field of study. We value the integrity, originality, and depth of knowledge of our authors.

Our readers are our most important resource, and we appreciate your input, suggestions, and ideas about what you would like to see published.

Visit our website at www.redwheelweiser.com to learn about our upcoming books and free downloads, and be sure to go to *www.redwheelweiser.com/newsletter* to sign up for newsletters and exclusive offers.

You can also contact us at *info@rwwbooks.com* or at

Red Wheel/Weiser, llc
665 Third Street, Suite 400
San Francisco, CA 94107